W9-AOM-906

MONTANA PLACES

MONTANA PLACES
Exploring Big Sky Country

JOHN B. WRIGHT
with a foreword by
Cotton Mather and George F. Thompson

NEW MEXICO GEOGRAPHICAL SOCIETY
MESILLA

This book is the second volume in the *Registered Places of America* series, published by the New Mexico Geographical Society of Mesilla, New Mexico, in cooperation with the Center for American Places, Harrisonburg, Virginia, and Santa Fe, New Mexico. The first volume, *Registered Places of New Mexico: The Land of Enchantment*, was published in 1995, and is distributed by the Center for American Places (www.americanplaces.org).

Copyright © 2000
New Mexico Geographical Society
All rights reserved

Printed in the
United States of America
First edition, 2000

Distributed by the University of
Minnesota Press, Minneapolis

Requests for permission to
reproduce material from this book
should be sent to the
NEW MEXICO GEOGRAPHICAL SOCIETY
P. O. BOX 1201
MESILLA, NEW MEXICO 88046-1201
U.S.A.

The acid-free paper used in this book
meets the minimum requirements
of American National Standard for
Information Sciences—Permanence
of Paper for Printed Library
Materials, ANSI Z39.48-1984.

A Cataloging-in-Publication record
for this book is available from the
Library of Congress.

All photographs are by the author,
except as noted.

ISBN 0-8166-3704-0
ISBN 0-8166-3705-9 pbk

Frontispiece:
Glacier National Park

Design and typography by
George Lenox Design, Austin

THIS "PLACE" CALLED MONTANA has been cyclically beaten, battered and bruised . . . But if the fight against environmental degradation can be won anywhere, it will be won here—precisely because nowhere else in America is that visceral relationship with the land more powerfully felt.

K. Ross Toole
Twentieth-Century Montana:
A State of Extremes (1972)

CONTENTS

IN ANOTHER BOOK, *Montana Ghost Dance: Essays on Land and Life,* author Jack Wright says: "For most of my twenty-five years in the state, all of Montana felt like prized troutwater. The most ethical thing to do was to keep quiet about it. But now, the place has been found by the rest of the world. Montana is being filmed, claimed, mined, settled, and misunderstood like never before. The cat's out of the bag."

Eight million people now visit Montana each year—summer, spring, winter, fall. Fellow citizens from North America and continents around the world are coming to Montana *like never before*—all with high hopes in "checking it out." As tourists, as entrepreneurs, as wannabe residents, as potential absentee landowners, these folks are seeking profit, pleasure, a really good time, and even perhaps a taste of self-discovery. Meanwhile, the long-time residents try to figure them out and what their impact will be on their beloved state.

Jack Wright could have selected and written about hundreds of places in Montana that, singularly and considered together, would make people say, "Ah, yes, that is what Montana is all about." But in inviting Jack to write this book, we asked that he limit his selection of special Montana places to thirty-one, in keeping with the guidelines of the series in which this book appears: *Registered Places of America.* Jack was asked to prepare a preliminary list of Montana places that, to him, deserve recognition and tribute and that, collectively, represent the state as a whole. He then submitted that list—comprising far more than thirty-one places—to us, as series founders and directors, and to the publisher's editorial advisory committee, for final approval. And it was from this list that the thirty-one Montana places included in this book were confirmed by one and all.

This was no easy task. Montana is a large state with a big-sized reputation and its own complex human and physical geography. It is both the Great Plains and Northern Rockies, for example; both reality and fantasy with a sense of a distinct homeland emerging. But the emphasis in this book, in keeping with the spirit of the series, is on the importance of *place* as an idea, and of comprehending the interconnectedness of our natural and humanly constructed worlds. Traditionally, society rewards the individual landmark as the truest indicator of the historic past. But *place* involves not only the individual points in a landscape, but also the relationships between them. It involves more than the historic hotel; it means a web, a continuum, of points that reveal a place. Thus, the Lolo Trail is a place, just as the river that runs through it is a place, just as the Rocky Mountain Front, High-Line, Paradise Valley, and Yellowstone are places.

Thus, it is with great pleasure and pride that we present *Montana Places: Exploring Big Sky Country* by the esteemed author Jack Wright. He has fulfilled his promise to uncover and reveal for us those thirty-one special places that represent and pay tribute to Montana—a state he obviously loves and knows inside out, as a scholar, writer, conservationist, and Missoula resident. Some of the places included are already listed on state and federal historic registers; all of the thirty-one places are now registered as well with the New Mexico Geographical Society and the Center for American Places as special places not only of Montana, but also of America.

It is our hope that you, the reader of *Montana Places*, will enjoy its pages, and its photographs, and benefit from its dual message: that Montana is a special place, comprised of many regions, geographies, and individual places, and that the quality of life in Big Sky Country depends increasingly on leadership, and the manner in which newcomers and old-timers alike care for its lands.

Cotton Mather and George F. Thompson
series founders and directors

THIS IS A BOOK ABOUT the geography of Montana, and geography is about place. The following pages examine the distinctive traits and meaning of thirty-one astonishing places in Big Sky Country.

I believe a single historic structure or geologic formation can take us only so far in understanding a state. To concentrate on single points is to miss the grand stories of land and life that swirl around these features. Readers of this book are encouraged to think about Montana as a whole.

Any particular place may have a special meaning for any particular person. But those meanings, taken one after another, can add up to larger understandings of our relationship to the humanly constructed and natural worlds in which we live, work, and visit. In those connections lie the idea—the meaning—of place.

Each portion of Montana has a unique look and feel. Somehow we just know when we've changed from one kind of geography to the next. This changing "sense of place" comes from all the rich and varied bonds between human beings and the lands we call home.

The lessons and tales of Montana registered places form the heart of this book. Following are descriptions of thirty-one "official places" registered with the New Mexico Geographical Society of Mesilla, New Mexico, which pioneered the concept along with the Center for American Places of Harrisonburg, Virginia. The sites mentioned in this book include some historic landmarks already listed on the National Register of Historic Places and many others that complement the Register.

Beyond their "official" standing, I have tried to convey the *geographical* importance of each place. In designating "places" that best tell the story of Montana, I took care to consider aspects of geography, history, environment, and culture. I have worked in and explored Montana since I first arrived here in 1973. In preparing this volume, I traveled the state all over again and talked to ranchers, scholars, writers, and other people to learn how they see the past and present landscapes. But what follows is a personal account written by someone who plainly loves this contentious, achingly beautiful state.

The sequence of registered places is neither alphabetical, temporal, nor regional. We begin with the buffalo jump known as Ulm Pishkun and move across the state in search of geographic variety, from Glacier National Park to Red Rock Lakes and Refuge. This was done to add interest to the order of presentation. There are two indexes at the end of the book: A general index with standard cross-references and a specific index for Montana's registered places.

Travelers to Big Sky Country will read about these places as they design and follow their own meanderings through the state. The book's format allows travelers to learn about where they are one place at a time. Readers who start at the beginning and proceed to the end of the book will notice some minor but necessary repetitions, such as the route of the Lewis and Clark Expedition.

I did not intend to present a complete overview of the state's history or geography. Neither did I feel compelled to include every major community in the state. Montana is far more than its cities. What follows is a distillation of what I believe are the most telling facts, observations, insights, and musings about some remarkable and important Montana places.

Many detailed guidebooks about the state are available, including the 1939 WPA guide, a wonderful roadside geology, and a helpful roadside history. I have also referenced other literature as guideposts to further reading.

It is my hope that by reading and thinking about the registered places of Montana, and by exploring them firsthand, readers will gain new insights into what Big Sky Country is *really* like. Montana is currently portrayed in national media as the next utopia, the next Colorado or California. Being physi-cally present in Montana can allow one to see Montana as it once was—a wild land crafted by raw, glorious forces. But we can also see the landscape of today—exploited still by mining, logging, and careless development and conserved in some small measure by the actions of good-hearted people. Montana is neither mythical nor pristine. It is a reality composed of both durable beauty and heartbreaking loss.

That is the message of *Montana Places.*

Jack Wright
Missoula, Montana
195 years after Lewis and Clark

ACKNOWLEDGMENTS

THIS BOOK PROJECT came from the energetic minds of Cotton Mather, president of the New Mexico Geographical Society, and George F. Thompson, president of the Center for American Places. I am grateful for the opportunity to contribute to their unique series, *Registered Places of America.*

In Montana, help came from the land itself and from scores of folks who truly know their state. Special thanks to Pat Bik of the Montana State Historic Preservation Office in Helena and the staff of the Mansfield Library at the University of Montana in Missoula.

Thanks, as always, to Jamie Kay of Fine Lines in Missoula, for superb editing and comments on several drafts of the manuscript.

Grateful appreciation is also extended to George Lenox of Austin, Texas, for his masterful book design.

Bravo to Kathi Olson for crafting the preliminary map of the state and for countless insights of real value for many years.

Many of the book's photographs were taken during my field visits. In the best interests of the reader, however, I used pictures taken by others when they were better than mine, for which I am grateful.

Gratitude to Joseph Kinsey Howard for writing the best book on the state: *Montana: High, Wide and Handsome* (1943).

Muchas gracias to Bethita.

Many thanks to Cathy for being a wonderful big sister.

This book is dedicated to my mother, Betty, who gave me a love of beautiful words and well-tended places.

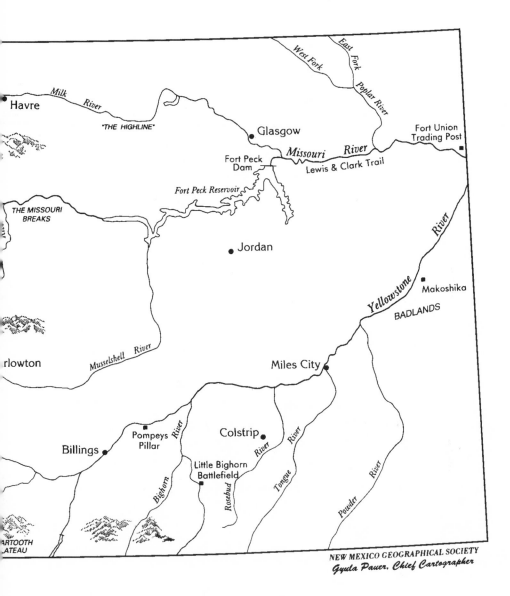

MONTANA

MONTANA IS BIG SKY COUNTRY an astonishing landscape of grasslands, badlands, rivers, and peaks. The state is so big that one image of the place is insufficient to reveal all of its true nature. In fact, geographers and residents alike rarely refer to Montana as a whole but prefer to speak of three separate regions within the state.

Western Montana is defined as the land lying west of the Continental Divide atop the Rocky Mountains. This landscape of high crestlines and narrow valleys lies entirely within the watersheds of the Clark Fork and Flathead rivers. It begins at Glacier National Park and extends south to Anaconda; it reaches west from the Bob Marshall Wilderness in the Flathead National Forest to the high ridgeline of the Bitterroot Mountain Range on the Idaho border. Missoula, at the confluence of the Blackfoot and Clark Fork rivers, is the region's largest city with a 1998 population of about 50,000. Its economy is based on wood products, tourism, retail trade, and the University of Montana.

Central Montana begins at the Continental Divide and extends eastward across a spacious landscape of broad valleys and spectacular island-like mountain ranges. The region spreads south from the Canadian border to the Beartooth Mountain Range and Yellowstone National Park. This terrain is home to the headwaters of the Missouri and Yellowstone rivers and includes a diverse mosaic of secondary watersheds once prized by fur trappers for beaver, mink, and otter. Today, cattle, sheep, hay, and grains are the leading exports. The largest city in Central Montana is Great Falls (1998 population about 57,000), and its economy is focused on agriculture, retail trade, Malmstrom Air Force Base, and tourism drawn to the site of Charlie Russell's home.

Eastern Montana sprawls across the remainder of the state to the borders of Canada, the Dakotas, and Wyoming. This rolling expanse of ranches and farms is more diverse than people expect, with badlands such as the Missouri Breaks and Makoshika State Park; wetland ecosystems along the Yellowstone, Missouri, and Bighorn rivers; and rimrock ledges dotted with pines. This is the "Big Open," the true Big Sky Country. Billings is the most populous city with a 1998 population of about 84,000 residents who work at jobs in oil and gas refining, transportation, trade, and the processing of agricultural products.

Although all maps of Montana depict the state's political boundaries, be assured Montanans perceive their territory as having three separate regions: Western, Central, and Eastern. Knowing this may be helpful when receiving directions to various sites in Big Sky Country.

Origin of Name: From the Spanish "Montaña,"
meaning "mountainous"
Area: 147,138 square miles, the fourth largest state
(only Alaska, Texas, and California are larger)
East-West extent: 535 miles
North-South extent: 275 miles
Highest Point: Granite Peak (12,799 feet) in the
Beartooth Mountains near Cooke City
Lowest Point: 1,820 feet where the Kootenai River
enters Idaho on US 2.
Mean Elevation: 3,400 feet
1960 Population: 674,767
1990 Population: 799,065
1998 Population: 880,000 (estimated)
Population Density (1990): 5.66 people per square mile
Average Number of Visitors per Year: 8 million
Number of Congressional Representatives: One
Notable Montanans: Gary Cooper (Helena), Chet Huntley
(Cardwell), Myrna Loy (Radersburg), and Jeannette Rankin
(Missoula), who, in 1916, was the first woman elected
to the national House of Representatives
Number of Electoral Votes: Three
Lowest Recorded Temperature: Minus 70 degrees Fahrenheit
at Rogers Pass on 20 January 1954 (also the record
low for the United States)
Highest Recorded Temperature: 117 degrees Fahrenheit
at Medicine Lake on 5 July 1937
Range of Recorded Temperatures: 187 degrees, the largest
range for any state (North Dakota is second with 181 degrees;
Alaska is third with 180 degrees)
Flathead Lake: 28 miles long, 8 to 15 miles wide, the
largest freshwater lake west of the Mississippi River
Major Cities and their 1990 and Estimated 1998 Populations:
Billings (81,151; 84,000), Great Falls (55,097; 57,000),
Missoula (42,918; 50,000), Butte (33,336; 35,000),
Helena (capitol city) (24,569; 26,000), Bozeman (22,660;
25,000), Kalispell (11,917; 14,000)
Major Indian Nations *(at the time of Lewis and Clark):*
Arapaho, Blackfeet, Cheyenne, Crow, Flathead,
Kootenai, *Pend d'Oreille, Salish,* Shoshone, and
Sioux (Lakota)

Principal Crops Raised: Spring and winter wheat, hay, oats, barley, sugar beets, corn, and potatoes

Principal Minerals Mined: Copper, silver, gold, zinc, and coal (also oil, gas, marble, and sapphires)

Date of Statehood: 8 November 1889; the forty-first state to enter the Union

State Nickname: The Treasure State

State Motto: Oro y Plata ("Gold and Silver")

State Flower: Bitterroot

State Tree: Ponderosa Pine

State Bird: Western Meadowlark

State Mammal: Grizzly Bear

Ulm Pishkun   MONTANA'S HUMAN GEOGRAPHY begins as the
Ice Age was ending. About 25,000 years ago, paleo-
Indians from Asia crossed the Bering Land Bridge into
North America. Most followed an ice-free corridor east
of the Canadian Rockies southward through Montana
along the Old North Trail. This trail extended south-
ward into Mexico. While some immigrants stayed in
Montana, most pushed onward.

The first "Montanans" were migratory hunters and
gatherers. Game was killed using sharp spear points
fashioned from obsidian (volcanic glass) or flint. By
about 8,000 years ago, human populations had grown,
and groups of hunters began to stalk bison using
communal tactics at places such as Ulm Pishkun, a
remarkable, windswept hunting ground located on
rimrock nine miles west of what is now Great Falls
near the quiet farming town of Ulm.

Bison were stampeded across the Plains toward
plateaus where stone drive lanes or natural topography
hemmed in the animals. The hunters ran behind
shouting. Their dogs barked and chased the frothing
beasts. Finally, the panicked animals were driven over
a rocky cliff called a pishkun. Many bison died. Indians
waited below to finish off the injured whose bodies lay
broken across knife-edged boulders. The carcasses
were butchered, and feasts were held with much
drumming and singing. Most of the flesh was dried
into jerky for the winter. Wolves, coyotes, eagles, and
other wildlife species cleaned up the rest.

Bison formed one of the practical and spiritual
foundations of life for paleo-Indians and recent tribes.
The meat, hides, horns, and bones of these great,
shaggy creatures sustained the hunters and their
families. Bison were part of the voice of the land.

Pishkuns (bison jumps or, as they are most often
called, "buffalo jumps") were used by American
Indians for thousands of years, yet the bison herds
remained vast. At the time of white settlement in
North America, more than 60,000,000 bison were
believed to have roamed in vast herds over much of
the landscape, especially the Great Plains. Market

**The bonepile at the cliff base was plundered in late-1940s
and 1950s for fertilizer. Sensing a vanished way of life on
the land is the challenge of Ulm Pishkun. Look over the
vast openness of grain fields and pastures extending to the
horizon. This was once a wild place—an ocean of unbroken
grassland. Imagine the landscape blackened by millions of
bison being stalked by skilled Indian hunters. Feel the
presence of their absence. Photograph courtesy of the
Montana Historical Society, Helena.**

hunting for hides, tongues, and bones began to deci-
mate the herds as settlement moved westward. By the
middle of nineteenth century, the bison were gone east
of the Mississippi River, and by 1900 only two wild
herds remained of about 2,000 bison each, one in
Yellowstone National Park and one in Canada. Today,
bison herds are being re-established in many parts of
America, especially in Montana, New Mexico, and
Nebraska. These strong-willed animals can be ob-

served in their natural habitat within the National Bison Range at Moiese in north-central Montana.

Ulm Pishkun is one of the largest buffalo jumps ever found. It is now a state park that offers the opportunity to feel ancient ways of land and life. Here, limestone, shale, and sandstone cliffs range from 15 to 30 feet high and extend for one-half mile. "Major" and "minor" kill sites have been unearthed by archaeologists. Seven other kill sites can be seen from the Park's overlook.

The pishkun was most intensively used from A.D. 650 until horseback hunting began around A.D. 1600. Countless layers of bison bones have been excavated at the cliff base. Artifacts such as arrowheads, stone knives, awls, scrappers, bone beads, drills, and choppers have been recovered. Trails and interpretive signs lead you through boulders, cheatgrass, and tumblemustard. A black-tailed prairie dog town covers much of the 170-acre Park. To assure Ulm Pishkun's protection, Ted Turner has purchased 1,080 acres of the adjacent rimrock.

FOR MORE ON BUFFALO:
The North American Buffalo,
by Frank Gilbert Roe (1972).

The Lewis and Clark Trail

THE LEWIS AND CLARK EXPEDITION traversed many portions of Montana in 1805 and 1806. The amazing stories of these mercantile adventurers are woven tightly into the geography of Big Sky Country. The Lewis and Clark Trail is not a single place. It is the route of an American odyssey to a "new" land. Travelers can still retrace many of the explorers' footsteps in Montana.

More than half of Montana was once part of "Louisiana," a vast area claimed by the French at the turn of the nineteenth century that stretched from the Mississippi River to the Rocky Mountains. President Thomas Jefferson's vision of Manifest Destiny demanded that the United States eventually extend to the Pacific Ocean. In April of 1803, an embattled Napoleon sold the 523-million-acre Louisiana Territory to the U.S. for a paltry $15 million. The national domain was instantly doubled in size.

The Lewis and Clark statue in Fort Benton with Francis O'Hara, retired grain farmer and rare find—a native Montanan.

In 1804, President Jefferson hired Captains Meriwether Lewis and William Clark of Virginia to lead a two year expedition through Louisiana to the Pacific Ocean. Their mission was to search out a land route to the Pacific, to strengthen American claims to the Oregon Territory, and to explore and record all they encountered—Indians, mountains, rivers, soils, plants, and animals (especially ones with fine fur pelts). Only $2,500 was provided for supplies.

Lewis and Clark and their party were trained in Illinois across the Mississippi from St. Louis, the expedition's starting point. In May of 1804, they moved up the Missouri River in canoes and pirogues (dug-out boats). They reached the mouth of the Yellowstone River in April of 1805. Traveling up the Missouri, they witnessed vast herds of bison, elk, and antelope. Grizzly bears were frequent visitors to their campsites.

Lewis and Clark paddled past tributary rivers they named the Milk, Musselshell, Judith, and Marias. One afternoon, a tall plume of mist rose ahead. It was the Great Falls of the Missouri where the city of Great Falls is now located. This was their first clear landmark, and Lewis acclaimed the falls as "the grandest sight I ever beheld."

The expedition portaged around the defile and canoed upstream past the steep limestone walls of a canyon they named "the Gates of the Rocky Mountains." Guided by a Shoshone Indian woman named Sacajawea (the Bird Woman), they soon reached the confluence of three great rivers which joined to form the Missouri. The site became known as "Three Forks." They named the rivers the Jefferson (for President Jefferson), the Madison (for Secretary of State James Madison), and the Gallatin (for Treasury Secretary Albert Gallatin), who, at the time, was establishing the National Road, America's first "interstate" highway which eventually extended from Baltimore to East St. Louis on the Mississippi River. Having paid their political debt, the Lewis and Clark party moved up the Jefferson River, crossed the Continental Divide on August 12th, and entered what is now Idaho.

Pompey's Pillar near Billings. Walkways lead to the top for a fine view. Photograph courtesy of the Montana Department of Commerce: Travel Montana.

In the Lemhi River country, Lewis and Clark met a band of the Shoshone Nation. These were Sacajawea's people. The explorers spoke with her brother, Chief Cameahuait, traded for horses, and headed north through Montana's Bitterroot Valley. Racing against the changeable weather of fall, the expedition made a laborious and nearly fatal crossing of the Bitterroot Mountains on the Lolo Trail. On the other side, the Nez Perce generously revived them with food.

Lewis and Clark then proceeded by boat down the Clearwater River to the Snake River and on to the fast-moving Columbia. They reached the Pacific on 7 November 1805. William Clark wrote: "Great joy in camp, we are in view of the Ocean, this great Pacific Ocean, which we have been for so long anxious to see."

In the spring of 1806, Lewis and Clark backtracked up the Columbia and crossed the Lolo Trail into Montana. Lewis took a small group, including two Nez Perce guides, up the Blackfoot Valley toward the Missouri River. Clark led a larger body down the Jefferson to Three Forks and crossed the Gallatin Valley (at present-day Bozeman) to the Yellowstone River. There they built dugout canoes and floated downstream toward the Bighorn, Tongue, and Powder rivers.

Near the current site of Billings, the group pulled their boats from the water and walked to an isolated sandstone rock. Indian petroglyphs (etchings) and pictographs (paintings) of animals and figures covered the walls. Captain Clark named this feature "Pompey's Pillar," in honor of Sacajawea's son, Pomp, and carved his name and the date (July 25th, 1806) in the rock. It can still be seen today.

Lewis and Clark arrived at the confluence of the Yellowstone and Missouri rivers within nine days of each other—an amazing feat in such remote country. It had been a peaceful journey except for a single conflict with the Blackfeet, during which Lewis shot an Indian to death. From their rendezvous site, the expedition drifted down the Missouri to the Mississippi and reached St. Louis on 23 September 1806.

The journals of Lewis and Clark caused a sensation. These were the first organized, systematic accounts of Louisiana, and the news was very good. Lewis and Clark had proven that unimaginable wealth in fur, timber, minerals, and farmland existed out in the "new lands." The captains proclaimed the upper Missouri "richer in beaver and otter than any other country on earth." In addition, the expedition had put to rest the myth of a riverine Northwest Passage and shored up U.S. claims to an area coveted by the British.

FOLLOWING ALONG:
Undaunted Courage: Meriwether Lewis, Thomas Jefferson, and the Opening of the American West, by Stephen E. Ambrose (1996) and *Along the Trail with Lewis & Clark,* by Barbara Fifer and Vicky Soderberg (1998).

The remarkable accomplishments of Lewis and Clark also alerted the Indians that white people, although still far away, would one day arrive in numbers greater than the stars in the sky. The Lewis and Clark Interpretive Center is now open at Great Falls.

Glacier National Park and Ecosystem

GLACIER NATIONAL PARK was established in 1910 to protect a striking landscape composed of exquisite landforms carved by glacial ice. Traversing the 1,013,000-acre-park on the Going to the Sun Road, visitors can see many classic cirques (basins formed at the head of alpine glaciers), tarns (glacial lakes in cirques), aretes (ridgelines), horns (peaks), cols (passes),

U-shaped valleys, and waterfalls. Although the Ice Age may be over, several small active glaciers still exist along the Continental Divide. The Sperry and Grinnell glaciers can be hiked to with some effort and great care. While the Lewis Range appears lofty, the highest point in the Park is only 10,438 feet at the summit of Mount Cleveland. The Colorado Rockies contain fifty-four peaks in excess of 14,000 feet. Perhaps Glacier's most unusual mountain is Triple Divide Peak whose waters drain west into the Pacific Ocean, east to the Gulf of Mexico, and north to Hudson Bay in Canada.

The flat-lying, reddish, green, tan, and maroon rocks that are seen throughout Glacier Park contain numerous surprises. Preserved in the mudstone, quartzite, and limestone strata are ripple marks and mud cracks from the shallow margins of an ancient sea dating to the Precambrian geologic era, some 1 billion years ago. Rain drops from ancient passing showers have left their impressions. In some layers, fossilized stromatolites (colonies of algae) can be seen.

The vegetation on the west side of Glacier is lush with thick forests of western red cedar, hemlock, Douglas fir, subalpine fir, and western larch. The western red cedar groves along Avalanche Creek are cool and moist, reminding many visitors of the Cascade Mountains. Logan Pass (6,654 feet), on the Going to the Sun Road, is above treeline. From the Visitors Center, a boardwalk leads out into the alpine meadows covered in swaths of yellow glacier lily. The snow is seldom completely gone before July 4th so be sure to grab one of the orange walking poles to ease your return trip across snow-covered sections of the trail. Bighorn sheep, mountain goats, and marmots are often seen here.

Descending to St. Mary's Lake, the forests re-appear but are more sparse in the "rainshadow" of the high ridgeline of the Continental Divide. On a rainy day in West Glacier, it is often possible to find sunshine in East Glacier. From here, you pass eastward through a belt of aspen groves to the Great Plains.

Early tourists to Glacier arrived by train on the Great Northern Railway. Many Glacier Lodge and the

Glacier National Park. Beargrass flowers and high peaks in the Many Glacier area. Photograph courtesy of the Montana Department of Commerce: Travel Montana.

The alpine boardwalk at Logan Pass. Photograph courtesy of the Montana Department of Commerce: Travel Montana.

**Bighorn sheep in Glacier. Photograph courtesy of the
Montana Department of Commerce: Travel Montana.**

Park's other hotels were built during this era. The Izzak Walton Inn at Essex on Glacier's south border is still served by daily trains. However, today most visitors arrive by car along U.S. Highway 2. The stretch of this road from Columbia Falls to the West Glacier entrance is now a smurge of helicopter rides, theme parks, waterslides, a tacky "House of Mystery," and sundry other tourist traps.

Glacier National Park is really an "island" surrounded by a sea of diverse and sometimes conflicting land uses. When the Park was formed, it was believed large enough to sustain its populations of grizzly bear, wolves, elk, bighorn sheep, bald eagles, and myriad other wildlife species. In the years since, a variety of external threats to the Park have proven that it is not.

Glacier is bordered on the east by the Blackfoot Indian Reservation where oil and gas development is occurring. Along the Park's south boundary, mining, forest harvesting, and oil and gas exploration are occurring in the Lewis and Clark National Forest. To the west are an aluminum smelter at Columbia Falls, forest clearcutting, ski resort development, and the intense sprawling expansion of Whitefish and Kalispell. Coal mining in Canada threatens to leak acids into the clear waters of the North Fork of the Flathead River. All of these external land uses place the Park at significant risk. Biologists already report increasing conflicts between the Park's grizzly bears, elk herds, and wolves and people in adjacent areas. In addition, record numbers of visitors to Glacier are creating various internal pressures on its natural beauty. The Park has more than 2 million visitors each year.

Glacier is much more than a single national park. It is part of a larger geography—the Greater Glacier Ecosystem—a vast expanse that embraces such lands as the 1,009,356-acre Bob Marshall, 285,701-acre Great Bear, and 239,936-acre Scapegoat wilderness areas. With proper stewardship of both the Park and surrounding places, this landscape always can remain a wild haven for the Great Bear—grizzly—and human beings wishing to fill their eyes with beauty.

TO REMEMBER THE PLACE:
Glacier National Park,
by David Rockwell (1995).

The Berkeley Pit is reached via Continental Drive exit off
Interstate 90. The Pit measures 1-1/2 miles long, a mile
wide, and 1,800 feet deep. Toxic mine acids mixed with
groundwater now form a lake 800 feet deep. This dangerous
broth is rising about two feet per month and is expected to
reach the top of the Pit by the year 2025. A celebration has
not yet been planned.

Butte   GOLD AND SILVER STRIKES evoke romantic,
gleaming images of the frontier. Yet, it was the dull red
metal known as copper that built Montana.

Butte is the rawboned, copper mining city where
modern Montana began. Historian Joseph Kinsey
Howard called the place the state's "black heart." It is
located beside the Continental Divide at an elevation
of 5,767 feet and is home to about 35,000 residents.
Butte is the state's most ethnically diverse community, with substantial numbers of Irish, Finns, Slavs,
Welsh, Italians, Cornish, Poles, and people from
dozens of other ancestries. These are mining families;
at least they were until the copper boom ended in the
1970s. And to understand Butte, the story of copper
must be told.

Butte began as a gold and silver camp. Copper was
seen as a "waste metal." In 1880, an Irishman named
Marcus Daly, who had previously helped develop the
Comstock Lode in Virginia City, Nevada, used $30,000
from San Francisco industrialists such as George
Hearst to buy a rather "unpromising" silver mine in
Butte called the "Anaconda." Little silver was found
but copper ore was found in deep shafts that assayed
out as 30 to 50% pure.

Daly began to buy up surrounding claims. He knew
that with the expansion of electric lighting, indoor
plumbing, and armaments manufacturing, copper was
a metal with a big future. Between 1882 and 1884, the
Anaconda Copper Mining Company shipped 37,000
tons of copper ore to smelters as far away as Swansea,
Wales, and still made a $2.5 million profit. Some of the
ore was even "open smelted" in Butte by building
alternating layers or ore and logs and setting the stack
on fire. Air pollution problems were extreme. Yet,
workers came from all over the world to toil in the
dangerous mine shafts spreading beneath the landscape. More than 100 structures called "head frames"
were built above shafts to lower miners more than a
mile below the surface. In 1884, a smelter was built
twenty-eight miles northwest of Butte, and a new
company town called Anaconda was created.

This head frame ("gallows frame") was once used to lower miners into the 5,000 miles of dangerous shafts and tunnels laying beneath Butte.

By 1890, the Butte copper mines were being called "The Richest Hill on Earth." More than 60 million pounds of copper were produced annually. Montana was then providing 43% of the country's copper, replacing Michigan as the nation's leader. The red metal was generating five times the wealth of gold in Montana. As a result of the mining boom, Montana's population soared from 39,000 in 1880 to 143,000 in 1890. The Butte/Anaconda area had expanded to more than 30,000 residents in twenty years. Saloons, dance

**"Copper King" William
Andrews Clark's Mansion,
built in 1888 at a cost of
$260,000. At the time, Clark
was personally earning $17
million per month. The
mansion is now Butte's best
known bed and breakfast
establishment.**

halls, bordellos, and opium dens competed with
churches for the attention of hard-working miners.

   While the 1890s was a decade of national economic
depression, Butte was an island of wealth to industrialists. The workers struggled, but Marcus Daly and his
main rival, William Andrews Clark, each amassed a
fortune, built immense copper companies, started
newspapers, and, in the true spirit of democracy,
bought the votes of state legislators. Their competition
for control of the copper industry and the state govern-

ment has been called the "War of the Copper Kings."
In 1894, the state was considering two choices for its
permanent capitol city: Helena (the "temporary"
capitol) and Anaconda. Daly spent $2.5 million
pushing for Anaconda, his company town. Clark spent
$400,000 campaigning for Helena, a place far away
from Daly's clutches. Both copper kings used their
newspapers to spread lies about each other. In the end,
Helena was chosen by the spare margin of 2,000 votes.
There was no recount.

World War I created a great demand for copper to
build tanks, ships, and artillery shells. As production
was increased and a flood of immigrants arrived,
working conditions became even more dangerous.
Following a national trend, the Butte Miners Union
(formed in 1893) began to see its power slip away.
Some workers, dissatisfied with low wages and unsafe
practices, joined the International Workers of the
World (i.w.w.), a Socialist union group known as the
"Wobblies." In 1914, violence between Anaconda
Company "goon squads," workers, and competing
unions led to a state of martial law. In the chaos, men
were shot to death, and the Miners Union Hall was
dynamited. By 1917, working conditions remained
poor, and union conflicts continued. A tragic fire in
the Speculator Mine incinerated 162 men. The Butte
miners went on strike, but the copper companies
starved them back to work. An i.w.w.. leader, Frank
Little, was lynched by company "police." No union
was recognized in Butte from 1917 until 1934.

The high grade copper ore was played out by the
1950s. Most of the remaining ore contained less than
1% copper, and huge volumes of ore were needed to
make a profit. In 1955, the Berkeley Pit was opened
just east of town. This open-pit mine was named for
the mining engineers from the University of California
at Berkeley who designed it. Gigantic shovels loaded
ore onto trucks with eleven-foot tires and hauling
capacities of 170 tons. Each ton of ore yielded ten
pounds of copper. Up to 50,000 tons were mined each
day and shipped by rail to be smelted in Anaconda. In
1963, a "concentrator" was built next to the pit to

increase the content of the ore to 25% prior to smelting.

The copper boom in Butte effectively ended during the 1970s. Worldwide prices fell due to a global copper glut, the increasing use of PVC plumbing, and the decreasing use of copper wire. In addition, in 1972 the Anaconda Company's copper holdings in Chile were nationalized, causing a huge corporate loss. In 1976, ARCO (Atlantic Richfield Company) bought "The Company" (as Montanans called it) and soon closed down operations in the state. In its history, the Berkeley Pit produced 20.8 billion pounds of copper, 96 million pounds of molybdenum, 90 million ounces of silver, and 3 million ounces of gold. Today, smaller amounts of these metals are being mined at the Southeast Berkeley Pit.

From high on the Continental Divide a ninety-foot-tall white statue called Our Lady of the Rockies looks down on Butte. This is a city with faith. Despite a population decline from 60,000 in 1920 to 33,000 today, Butte survives. "Uptown Butte" is a National Historic District containing scores of intriguing structures such as the Metals Bank on Broadway, William Andrews Clark's mansion at 219 West Granite, and Charles Clark's Victorian "Art Chateau" at 321 West Broadway. Slag heaps, mine shafts, head frames, mill yards, and scenes of fascinating environmental devastation surround the city. Many areas of Butte are hazardous waste "Superfund sites" of the EPA (Environmental Protection Agency) in need of clean up. The World History of Mining located next to Montana Tech at the west end of Park and Granite streets is a must for enthusiasts of ore extraction.

Butte has the most raucous St. Patrick's Day in Montana. The "Butte Irish" have not forgotten how to celebrate. Scores of neighborhood bars are scattered throughout the city in ethnic neighborhoods. Former miners and descendants of miners fill many of the seats. Most have nicknames such as Old Buck, Mick, Dirty Bill, Slimy, and Angle Iron Mike. It is from these men that the real story of Butte, both heroic and heartbreaking, can be learned for the price of a draft beer or two.

FOR THE REST OF THE STORY:
The Battle for Butte,
by Michael P. Malone (1981).

The Blackfoot River   "IN OUR FAMILY, there was no clear line between religion and trout fishing." That is the classic opening sentence of *"A River Runs through It and Other Stories,"* Norman Maclean's novella about the Blackfoot. Robert Redford's 1995 movie based on this story was elegant, graceful, and geographically misleading.

The real river that runs through it is today an industrial watershed that is plagued by sediments washing down from clearcut forest slopes, mine acid leakage, and expanding housing development. Even the trout fishery, which formed the core of Maclean's tale, is so weakened that the Blackfoot River could not even play itself in Redford's movie. What you saw was actually filmed hundreds of miles away on five other rivers.

The Blackfoot River flows westward across Montana from the Continental Divide to its confluence with the Clark Fork River five miles upstream of Missoula. Route 200 follows the river. It can be followed eastward through the Garnet Mountains from Bonner, at the river's mouth, for ninety-two miles to Rogers Pass atop the Continental Divide at 5,610 feet. The Rocky Mountain Front and Great Plains lay beyond.

Indian hunting parties, Lewis and Clark, and scores of trappers and prospectors once passed through the watershed. However, it wasn't until Marcus Daly's Anaconda Company began copper operations in Butte and Anaconda (see pages 16 and 103) that the Blackfoot drainage began to be exploited seriously. In its heyday, the Washoe Smelter in Anaconda required 300,000 cords of fuel wood per year. Butte needed mine timbers and boards for all types of construction. Daly acquired vast amounts of this wood from the steep slopes rising above the Blackfoot. Some of this came from Anaconda holdings, but timber was poached from federal Forest Reserves by outfits such as the Missoula-based Montana Improvement Company. The Blackfoot began to be filled with log drives. Sedimentation increased. Over the years, the Clark Fork River became so polluted by the runoff from the Butte/Anaconda

The Blackfoot, the real river that runs through it. A massive gold mine near Lincoln threatens to destroy this already damaged river ecosystem.

copper complex that it ran red and orange as far downstream as Missoula. The entire Clark Fork watershed is now an EPA Superfund Site—the largest toxic waste cleanup project in the United States. The mouth of the Blackfoot is included.

The worst damage to the Blackfoot forests came during the 1970s and 1980s. Champion International Corporation acquired the Anaconda Company holdings and carried out an unprecedented clearcutting campaign. The logs were processed at the sawmill complex at Bonner/Milltown. About seven miles upstream from Bonner is a tributary called Gold Creek. A drive up this side canyon reveals the massive scale of Blackfoot clearcutting. Champion has moved on, and these same lands are now being exploited by Stimson Lumber.

During the 1960s and 1970s the watershed began to be subdivided and developed for recreational and residential homesites. To halt this damage, zoning restrictions, federal Wild and Scenic River designation, and many other options were considered by local residents. In the end, The Nature Conservancy (TNC), Montana Department of Fish Wildlife and Parks, the Montana Land Reliance, and Missoula County created an innovative, nationally-recognized program to protect the Blackfoot river corridor. The cornerstone involves having landowners voluntarily donate perpetual "conservation easements" that prohibit subdivision to TNC and other groups. To date, some 8,000 riverside acres have been protected in this way. River access is provided to the public across private lands at designated points. Irresponsible behavior by recreationists, however, will result in the closure of the access sites. Signs have been erected throughout the drainage explaining the rules.

The latest threat to the Blackfoot River is a massive gold mining operation being proposed near Lincoln by Canyon Resources, Inc. Some 208 million tons of low-grade ore will be taken from immense open-pit mines. A ton of ore will produce only 0.025 ounces of gold. Engineers estimate a yield of 5.2 million ounces of gold from the McDonald Meadows/Keep Cool deposit. Processing involves heaping ore on sealed pads where cyanide is applied to leach out the gold. Leaching pads will be built a quarter mile from the Blackfoot River. There is cause for concern. In 1975, a small dam failed on Mikehorse Creek (a tributary near Rogers Pass) where ASARCO had mined gold years before. More than 300,000 tons of tailings were moved by the creek and a plume of heavy metals and mine acids killed thousands of rainbow, brown, and cutthroat trout in the Blackfoot River. The river above Lincoln has never fully recovered.

Whether the mine is developed or not, the Blackfoot is constantly under an array of development pressures. The pristine river of our imaginations does not exist.

ESSENTIAL READING:
*A River Runs through It
and Other Stories,*
by Norman Maclean (1976).

In *A River Runs through It and Other Stories,* Norman Maclean concluded with the line "I am haunted by waters." The Blackfoot River is a haunting reminder of the difficulties Montanans face in conserving Big Sky Country.

Jordan JORDAN IS THE most remote county seat in the lower forty-eight states. This bare-boned cowtown, located thirty-one miles from Sand Springs (population 19), is the focus of life for the 1,589 far-flung residents of Garfield County. Just beyond Jordan's last trailer house is a silence so complete it roars in your ears. This community of 494 residents seems an unlikely place for one of the loudest debates over the future of the Western landscape: A proposal to return vast tracts of land into a "Buffalo Commons."

The undulating High Plains around Jordan were densely homesteaded during the 1909 to 1920 grain-farming boom in Montana. Drought, isolation, and soils so poor you couldn't "raise hell on a gallon of whiskey" soon led to a mass exodus. Tarpaper shacks, sod houses, and adobe dwellings made from local "gumbo clay" were abandoned to the elements. Some of these ruins still dot the countryside. The economy shifted to raising cattle on big spreads.

Yet, the remoteness continued to close in on those who stayed behind. By 1930, only eight of the county's 1,077 ranches had indoor plumbing. A few shortwave radios (powered by generators) were the only means of contact with the outside world. Electrical service wasn't established in Jordan until 1931. Phone lines would come five years later. Many rural ranches weren't hooked up to either until the 1940s.

Jordan remains one of Montana's most far and away places. The Garfield County High School is located near "downtown." Until 1995, this was Montana's only public school dormitory. Due to falling enrollment, students from distant ranches now stay in

The dormitory of the Garfield County High School in Jordan.

private homes in town to avoid daily round-trip commutes of up to 130 miles.

Jordan is a cowtown full of familiar, weather-worn faces. Strangers are as obvious to locals here as (in one resident's words) "a cow chip in a punchbowl." Jordan's stores and bars give residents a welcome chance to talk to someone other than their families or hired hands. The presence of satellite dishes, the availability of movie rentals, and the promise of regular trips to Miles City or Billings have done little to alter the people of this conservative cultural island. In 1996, a group of self-proclaimed "Freemen" retreated to a 960-acre ranch they called "Justus Township," where they held off FBI officials and other law enforcement agents for eighty-one days. These anti-government radicals disavowed the American monetary and legal systems and had a history of making threats to public officials.

Eight miles west of Jordan is another baffling site. Crystals of armalcolite have been found in the 50-million-year-old volcanic dikes of Smokey Butte. This fine-grained mineral was found in rocks brought back from the moon. It has never been found anywhere else on Earth but Smokey Butte. Jordan is now a place of both geological and cultural extremes.

The landscape around Jordan was once the home of bison and grizzly bear. By the 1870s, the bison were nearly extinct in the Plains. In 1886, the Smithsonian Institution sent William T. Hornaday to acquire specimens of this vanishing species for its museum. His party made camp near Sand Springs where twenty bison were killed. Taxidermists reassembled the skins and skeletons back in Washington where they caused quite a stir. Hornaday was a vocal advocate of bison conservation and was responsible for the creation of the National Bison Range in Montana's Flathead Valley in 1908.

The Big Open. A small group (right center) gathers at the place where the Hornaday bison hunting party camped in 1886. Photograph courtesy of the Montana State Historic Preservation Office.

Recently, conservationists made a bold proposal to return much of the Northern Great Plains to a natural state known as the "Big Open." There are many variations, but the basic idea is to re-create the wild "Buffalo Commons" landscape of the mid-nineteenth century. Sound farfetched?

The populations of counties such as Garfield (1,589), McCone (2,276), and Petroleum (516) are small and declining. Much of the land is already held by the State of Montana and federal agencies. Foreclosures have placed hundreds of thousands of acres in the hands of banks back east. Advocates of the "Big Open" believe that the land will empty one way or another, either by economic collapse or by the careful creation of a new kind of national park. The return of a portion of North America to pre-settlement conditions would not come easy. The ecological, political, and economic challenges would be immense. Perhaps the biggest barrier of all will be the proud ranchers who work in the wind below infinite big skies. Most would rather be gutshot than see this "damned out-of-stater nonsense" come true.

If you visit Jordan, by all means pause for some fried chicken, jo jo potatoes, and a beer at the Hell Creek Bar. Just don't use the phrase "Big Open" or mention the Freemen standoff. Play a George Strait tune on the jukebox, drink up, and move on.

TO STIR THINGS UP:
Where the Buffalo Roam,
by Anne Matthews (1992).

Fort Benton

FORT BENTON is a small Missouri River town born of the fur trade and built by the power of the steamboat. For three decades, it was one of the world's most inland ports—3,000 miles by river from the Gulf of Mexico. Today, it is a pleasant ranching and tourist town.

Beginning in the 1830s, the American Fur Company extended its influence upstream from Fort Union on the Dakota border. In 1847, Alexander Culbertson created a new fort at the head of navigation on the Missouri. It was named in honor of Senator Thomas Hart Benton of Missouri, whose political influence often helped the company. When Fort Benton was completed in 1854, it was a massive wood and adobe structure about 250-feet-square. It contained an inner courtyard and a two-story blockhouse but lacked the stockade and grand furnishings of Fort Union. Beaver pelts and bison hides were traded here for years. However, Fort Benton's most important role in the creation of Montana was yet to begin.

In 1859, Army Captain John Mullan arrived in Fort Benton with road-building engineers and scores of troops. His assignment was to construct a wagon road to the Pacific Northwest for use in the Indian wars. When this crude track was completed three years later, it extended all the way from Fort Benton to Fort Walla Walla in eastern Washington. The "Mullan Road" was never of much military importance but set the stage for what came next.

The steamboat "Chippewa" reached Fort Benton in 1859. It was the first of the flat-bottomed, double-engined vessels to make it this far upriver. The Missouri River is a dangerous mosaic of shifting

The Fort Benton Stockade in riverfront park.

The Fort Benton landing on the Missouri River is a favorite rock-skipping place for local kids.

Fort Benton: A perfect place for a river walk.

channels, sand bars, tree snags, and roiling whirlpools. The success of the Chippewa encouraged the captains of other steamboats to make the "Spring Run" upriver during high water.

Fort Benton was transformed into a transportation hub and mercantile pivot point between factories back east and Montana's mining frontier. Each boat brought some 400 tons of freight to the town's burgeoning collection of docks and warehouses. Freight wagons and stagecoaches were then loaded with supplies and sent racing off to make deliveries at Bannack, Helena, Virginia City, and other booming gold camps. Hoards of "greenhorn" prospectors also came upriver and dashed along the Mullan Road in search of gilded fortunes.

The spring of 1867 was the peak of the steamboat era. Thirty-nine boats arrived at Fort Benton, and 10,000 passengers walked off gangplanks into the boisterous dockside clutter. The "tenderfoot" joined a crush of merchants in broad-clothed coats, rivermen in

Statue in Fort Benton's riverfront park: "Shep's Vigil" (Grand Union Hotel in background). In 1936, a dying shepherd came into town with his mixed-breed dog, Shep. The man died quickly, and his body was sent "Back East" by train. Shep waited loyally by the tracks for years greeting each arriving train hoping his master would return. Finally, on a snowy day in 1942, Shep ran toward an incoming train, slipped, and was killed under its wheels. More than 400 people attended the funeral of this exemplary being.

sashes, buckskin-clad trappers, bullwhackers, muleskinners, and Indians. The steamboat traffic was extremely lucrative. Each passenger paid a hefty $150 for the trip from St. Louis to this remote place. In 1867 alone, passenger tickets generated $1.5 million dollars for the steamboat companies with freight charges adding untold additional revenues. A single trip to Fort Benton could yield $40,000 to $65,000 in profit—a fortune in those days.

Fort Benton was prospering. The elegant Choteau House was built in 1868 on Front Street as a fine hotel for river-lagged visitors. Stores were quickly stocked with the latest tools, soft goods, and fineries. During the 1870s and 1880s, the Baker family operated the largest mercantile business in Montana here. The family's aggressive trading forays into Canada caused the head of the Hudson's Bay Company to complain— "they have cut our dividends from pounds to shillings." In 1882, the brick Italianate-style Grand Union Hotel was added to the expanding riverside commercial district. It was called the "Waldorf of the West." Fort Benton was calling itself the "Chicago of the Plains" and had become a place of national attention.

Completion of the Great Northern Railroad to Helena in 1887 ended Fort Benton's prominence. Missouri River transportation had become antiquated. The last steamboat whistled its arrival at Fort Benton in 1922. By then, the rails had long-since claimed center stage.

Fort Benton is now a town of 1,660 farmers, ranchers, and merchants. Visitors can tour the ruins of the Fort's blockhouse and a museum in the city park. An agricultural museum is located three blocks to the west. Be sure to stroll along Front Street through the National Historic District. Picnic in the riverfront park. Visit the MacLeish, Conrad, and Baker houses, the nineteenth-century hotels, and the old fire house/ city hall. Walk out on the old iron river bridge and sit on one of the wooden benches. Watch the water wind downstream. Imagine the smokestacks and paddle-wheel spray of a steamboat coming around a cotton-wood bend.

OF RELATED INTEREST:
Montana's Missouri River,
Montana Geographic Series
(1979).

Colstrip   COLSTRIP IS ONE of America's most accurately
named town. This planned, energy-based community
has been the center of coal strip-mining in Eastern
Montana for more than seventy years. Colstrip is in
Rosebud County, twenty-seven miles south of Interstate 94 on Route 39.

In 1924, the Northern Pacific Railroad began strip-
mining coal from beneath the Montana grasslands.
Explosives were used to blast apart huge sections of
the landscape. Immense draglines and steam shovels
removed the "overburden" of soil and rock to expose
seams of sub-bituminous coal. The coal was then
loaded onto rail cars and shipped to locomotive
refueling stations. The small, functional town of
Colstrip sprang up with several brick and wood frame
storefronts.

In 1958, the Northern Pacific Railroad switched to
diesel fuel to power its engines and sold their extensive coal reserves to the Montana Power Company
(MPC). However, because of low demand, mining
activities stalled. By 1968, only 100 coal miners were
employed in the state.

The Northwest Central Power Study of 1971
changed everything. This report concluded that: (1)
Montana had 13% of U.S. coal reserves, (2) energy
demand was about to explode due to oil shortages, and
(3) a total of twenty-one coal-fired electrical generating
plants should be built in Eastern Montana. A coal rush
broke out, and leases were bought up for every square
foot of federal, state, and private lands thought to have
coal potential. With a ton of Montana coal replacing
3-1/2 barrels of expensive foreign (OPEC) oil, the
Colstrip area was called "America's Persian Gulf."

Big Sky Country was thrown into turmoil. Environ-
mentalists, ranchers, educators, and government
leaders warned the public that Eastern Montana was
about to become a "National Sacrifice Area." The
Northern Plains Resource Council cautioned that
strip-mining and coal-fired power plants would destroy
the environment and leave communities destitute
after the boom collapsed. Despite assurances by the
utility companies, most Montanans feared the coal

Colstrip 1 and 2 stacks on the left, 3 and 4 on the right. The massive scale of this Montana Power Company operation defies capture on film.

rush would cause air pollution, contamination of groundwater with mine acids, and the loss of plant and animal communities. In 1971, the state legislature passed the Major Facility Siting Act and the Montana Environmental Policy Act to protect the ecology of the Great Plains. In 1975, a Coal Severance tax was voted into law that required energy companies to pay 30% of their mining receipts into a state trust fund to assist towns with schools, parks, and economic development. This was the highest severance tax in the nation. The coal tax has since been reduced, and, to the dismay of conservationists, the $500 million fund is being spent by the state on a variety of short-term construction projects.

Western Energy's Rosebud Strip-Mine at Colstrip. At the top, a dragline works a seam; below, a shovel loads coal into a hauler. Photograph courtesy of Western Energy and the Montana Power Company.

Today, despite grand plans for twenty-one power plants, only four electrical generating facilities have been built in Eastern Montana: All at Colstrip. Colstrip 1 and 2 were completed in 1976. Each of these 333-megawatt power plants has a stack 507 feet tall. Colstrip 3 and 4 were brought on-line in 1986. These twin 776-megawatt giants have stacks rising 692 feet above the plains to distribute the emissions over a wider area. Both plants burn pulverized coal. Units 1 and 2 consume 2.8 million tons annually brought in by coal trains. Units 3 and 4 burn 6.4 million tons each year that is fed into their boilers from a four-mile-long covered conveyor belt system originating at the nearby Rosebud strip-mine.

Montana's mines now produce about 33 million tons of coal annually, a five-fold increase since 1971. Much of it is sub-bituminous coal with a low sulphur content (0.7%). This type of coal is preferred by utilities striving to meet federal clean air standards. Montana Power Company (through its Western Energy subsidiary), Westmoreland Resources, Peabody Coal, and the Decker Coal Company are the principal corporations involved. They acquire more than 60% of their coal from leases on U.S. Bureau of Land Management holdings. Since 1968, Western Energy has strip-mined about 10,400 acres in Eastern Montana, sixteen square miles. About half of this (4,200 acres) has been reclaimed and re-vegetated. More than half of that has now been returned to livestock grazing. Although earlier reclamation efforts often failed, today strip-mined lands usually can be healed. However, since coal beds act as groundwater aquifers, acids from strip-mines have affected springs, creeks, and agriculture in localized areas.

Electricity generated at Colstrip is "wheeled" (transmitted) by 1,200-kilovolt power lines across Western Montana to Seattle, Portland, and Los Angeles. Montana is a major exporter of energy. Critics of the Colstrip project call the state a "Resource Colony." Others see the development as an economic necessity since Eastern Montanans need jobs and receive most of their consumer goods from other regions. Western and Central Montanans are concerned that future power plants will require the construction of additional transmission lines across their wild, mountainous portion of the state. Nearly everyone agrees that diverting much of the Yellowstone River to slosh pulverized coal out of state through a slurry pipeline would be ecologically and economically damaging. Colstrip is a well-planned "company town" with 3,035 residents. The Montana Power Company and Western Energy have drawn the curtain on the ramshackle days. This is now a comfortable community where modest frame houses and trailers mix with parks, schools, modern shopping centers, and a challenging eighteen-hole golf course. Yet, there is only one reason everyone is here—jobs.

Montana ranks first in the nation in coal reserves with an estimated 120 billion tons still in the ground. At current rates of extraction from existing pits, mining could continue for another sixty years. Colstrip may be one boom town that lasts. But what will happen to the landscape if all the state's remaining coal reserves are mined? The Montana Coal Council estimates this would take 4,000 years at present levels of strip-mining. Even with our best of intentions, it is difficult to imagine that Montana's delicate grasslands could survive another forty centuries of mining.

READ WITH CAUTION:
The Rape of the Great Plains,
by K. Ross Toole (1976).

Beartooth Plateau and Range

THE BEARTOOTH PLATEAU is the most extensive landscape of alpine meadows and lakes in Montana. It is the state's Switzerland and the land of little summer.

The "Beartooth Highway" (U.S. 212), southwest of Billings, provides a sixty-four-mile-long grand traverse of this spectacular high country from Red Lodge to Cooke City. The Plateau is a gigantic block of three-billion-year-old gneiss (granite altered by heat and pressure). These are some of the oldest rocks on Earth. Greenland has the oldest at 3.8 billion years. The entire Beartooth massif has been uplifted along deep faults along its borders. Ice Age glaciers formed an ice cap over the Plateau and scoured it into rolling topography dotted with scores of sparkling blue lakes. Isolated rocky summits, such as Granite Peak (12,799 feet), frame the Plateau. Granite Peak in the Beartooth Range is the highest point in Montana.

From Red Lodge—once a coal-mining camp that today relies economically on tourism, recreation, and some agriculture—U.S. 212 rises sharply along a series of switchbacks before reaching Beartooth Pass (10,940 feet) astride the Montana/Wyoming border. The pass is often closed until June by snow depths of up to thirty

On top of the world in the Beartooth Plateau, a place of spectacular peaks, colorful alpine meadows, and frigid lakes. Photograph courtesy of the Greater Yellowstone Coalition.

feet. Much of the Plateau remains snow-covered until mid-July. Beartooth Pass is one of the best points of entry into the remote and rugged 944,060-acre Absaroka-Beartooth Wilderness Area. Twenty-eight peaks within "the Beartooth" rise to 10,000 feet elevation or higher. Hiking trails (about 700 miles of them) traverse the beautiful alpine landscape. Polygons of patterned ground can be seen in the meadows. The freezing and thawing of wet soil create these intriguing web-like patterns. The numerous lakes (nearly 1,000) yield few fish because of shallow depths and persistent ice covers. In August, the meadows are awash in pink moss campion, yellow sulphur flower, blue forget-me-not, and swaths of red and lavender dwarf alpine flowers. Summer is also the season when

A male wolf released in Yellowstone in 1994 was illegally shot and killed near Red Lodge, Montana a few months later. His mate was left to raise a litter of pups alone. Amazingly, wolves are still widely feared despite no recorded cases of attacks on people and only minor losses of livestock. Photograph courtesy of the Greater Yellowstone Coalition.

FOR MORE ON THE YELLOWSTONE WOLVES: *Wolf Wars,* by Hank Fischer (1995).

grizzly bears are most active in "The Beartooth." "Griz" regularly move between the wilderness and adjacent Yellowstone National Park. Also present in the Wilderness are bighorn sheep, mountain goats, elk, and moose. Nearby is the Grasshopper Glacier, named for the millions of frozen grasshoppers found imbedded in its ice. Each summer, grizzlies gather at its terminus to devour the insects as the glacier melts.

Heading west from Beartooth Pass, the highway continues into Wyoming for thirty-six miles. It re-enters Montana at Colter Pass (8,000 feet) near the hamlet of Cooke City. This tiny tourist community began as a mining camp in the 1880s.

The Beartooth Plateau and Range is a vital section of the Greater Yellowstone Ecosystem. In 1995, just southwest of Cooke City, gray wolves were reintroduced into Yellowstone Park. These elegant animals may one day be heard filling Beartooth nights with eery, marvelous howls. In this wild, elemental landscape, nothing could be more perfect and true.

Paradise Valley and Yellowstone

PARADISE IS AN APPROPRIATE NAME for the Yellowstone River Valley. U.S. 89 traverses the fifty-seven miles from Yellowstone National Park in Wyoming north to the railroad town of Livingston. The river is rated a Class I fishery, a national treasure of rainbow, brown, and cutthroat trout. The rugged peaks of the Absaroka-Beartooth Wilderness rise to the east culminating with Emigrant Peak at an elevation of 10,921 feet. To the west, the Gallatin Range is capped by Hyalite Peak (10,299 feet). Volcanic rocks some 45 to 55 million years old dominate the region's geology. Petrified trees are found in the Gallatin Petrified Forest up Rock Creek near Miner. Southward, Yellowstone National Park is the wild source of the Yellowstone River. The Park is a huge volcanic caldera famous for its geysers, hot springs and pools, canyons, waterfalls, and wildlife such as bison, elk, moose, swans, eagles, and grizzly bears. It is no wonder that a succession of people have tried to claim the Paradise Valley.

The first Europeans to see the Paradise region were fur trappers and explorers such as John Colter. In 1807, he witnessed the natural wonders of the Yellowstone area. Few believed his stories, and the region was known as "Colter's Lie" or "Colter's Hell." By the 1840s, Jim Bridger and other mountain men were crossing the geyser basins. Their accounts of features such as the Old Faithful geyser were dismissed as tall tales. These high-smelling men would soak in the hot springs of the Paradise Valley at the present site of the Chico Hot Springs Resort near Emigrant. Today, Chico has a large outdoor pool fed by the springs, spartan hotel rooms, and a gourmet restaurant.

In 1870, the Washburn-Langford Expedition traversed the valley and ascended the Yellowstone Plateau. These explorers confirmed through photographs and scientific measurements that all of Colter's and Bridger's stories were true. The nation was amazed, and Washington acted quickly to protect this astonishing landscape. Yellowstone National Park (2.2 million acres) was created in 1872 as the world's first national park.

Opposite: A Paradise Valley scene with Emigrant Peak and the Yellowstone River.

The main Church Universal and Triumphant complex beside the Yellowstone River at Corwin Springs. Modular homes seen here were purchased by CUT from the Bhagwan Shree Rasneesh when his utopian community in Oregon collapsed.

The community of Gardiner (5,287 feet; 670 residents) forms the south gateway into Yellowstone. This plain tourist town has numerous motels, shops, restaurants, and art galleries. To enter the Park you pass beneath the stone Roosevelt Arch which was dedicated by Teddy Roosevelt in 1903. Inscribed at the top are the words "For the Enjoyment of the People."

South of the Park beside u.s. 89 is the Devil's Slide. This bright red, vertical rock strata is composed of Triassic shale 180 million years old. The adjacent Cinnabar Mountain was misnamed, there is no cinnabar here (a source of mercury). Farther south is the narrow Yankee Jim Canyon. During the 1870s, an enterprising fellow named James George built the first road to Yellowstone Park and erected a tollgate which operated until 1883.

Today, the Paradise Valley is one of Montana's least peaceful places. Conflicts between ranchers, celebrities, developers, conservationists, and a religious cult known as the Church Universal and Triumphant are growing. The valley has been found by Hollywood celebrities such as Meg Ryan, Dennis Quaid, and Peter Fonda. Land subdivision is increasing along with soaring property values and taxes.

Groups such as the Rocky Mountain Elk Foundation have protected thousands of acres in the Paradise Valley that serve as key winter range habitats for the 9,000 elk of Yellowstone's "Northern Herd." Despite the grand size of the park, the surrounding private lands of the Greater Yellowstone Ecosystem play vital roles in its continuing survival. The State of Montana kills bison straying outside Park boundaries. Most ranchers fear these creatures may carry brucellosis, a disease that potentially threatens cattle, so they favor such shootings. Conservationists say the threat of infection is minimal and oppose killing the animals.

Even the Yellowstone River itself has come under attack. In the 1960s and 1970s, several proposals were made to build a dam at a site near Livingston known as Allenspur that would back water up into the Paradise Valley. The Yellowstone is the last undammed, major river in the lower forty-eight states. Thus far, conservationists have prevented this dam from being constructed.

The most peculiar threat to the Paradise Valley comes from a cult known as the Church Universal and Triumphant (CUT). In 1981, this group bought the 13,000-acre Royal Teton Ranch at Corwin Springs from publisher Malcolm Forbes. Today, the church owns some 30,000 acres in the valley and has created two massive subdivisions near Emigrant called Glastonbury North and South. The main ranch center is at Corwin Springs. This can be seen across the river from the CUT restaurant, the Ranch Kitchen. The charismatic leader of CUT is Elizabeth Clare Prophet. Her theology is a confusing blend of New Age mysticism, astrology, Christianity, reincarnation, yoga, anti-communism, and the legends of King Arthur and

Atlantis. The church claims 300,000 members world-wide, but the Paradise Valley is home to some 1,000 of the most ardent believers. The Church Universal and Triumphant is an apocalyptic sect which awaits a nuclear Armageddon. The Royal Teton Ranch has a bomb shelter which can house 756 people for seven years. Prophet's former husband, Edward Francis, spent time in federal prison on gun-running charges. Many local people fear that violence could occur here as in the cases of Jim Jones in Guyana or David Koresch in Waco, Texas.

The central lesson of the Paradise Valley is that utopia—a perfect place—will always lay beyond our grasp.

YOU WON'T BELIEVE IT:
Lords of the Seven Rays,
by Mark L. Prophet and
Elizabeth Clare Prophet
(1986).

Virginia City

VIRGINIA CITY is one of the West's most faithfully preserved placer mining towns of the 1860s gold boom. It sets at an elevation of 4,930 feet, fourteen miles west of Ennis on Route 287. Few of the 250,000 annual visitors are aware that the National Trust for Historic Preservation recently listed Virginia City as America's eleventh most endangered place. Its birth was just as dramatic.

In the spring of 1863, the enormously rich Alder Gulch-Virginia City placer deposits created Montana's most intense gold rush. Hoards of would be million-aires headed to this spot on the divide between the Tobacco Root and Gravelly ranges. A new townsite was laid out that was originally called Varina, in honor of the wife of Confederate President Jefferson Davis. However, these pro-Dixie sentiments were soon overruled, and the community was renamed Virginia City. Eight months later, it had 500 dwellings, stores, saloons, and other buildings. A series of gold camps called Adobetown, Junction, Nevada, Summit, Pine Grove, and Highland erupted along Alder Creek and the Ruby River. By 1864, the Virginia City area had 30,000 residents.

The town of Bannack's crooked Sheriff, Henry Plummer, managed to get his authority extended to include Virginia City. In the absence of a strong federal presence, "the law" tended to be improvised, and justice was immediately in short supply. Sheriff Plummer was informed of the schedules of gold, cash, and freight shipments. He passed the dates and routes on to his gang which then rode out and stole everything they could haul away. More than 100 people were murdered by Plummer's natural-born killers in a few months.

The miners and merchants of Virginia City responded by enlisting 2,000 local men as vigilantes to stop the road agents' reign of terror. Between January 4th and February 3rd of 1864, the vigilantes tracked down twenty-four men and hung them on the spot. Two weeks later, Sheriff Plummer and his inner circle of henchmen were arrested, quickly tried in "Miner's Court," and hung. Boone Helm, a particularly vicious louse, was reported to have said just before the noose broke his neck: "Kick away, old fellow. I'll be with you in Hell in a minute. Let her rip!" The Plummer threat had been snuffed out. Yet, peace came with a heavy cost. Several innocent men were hanged by the vigilantes in their rush to judgment.

Hydraulic mining came to Alder Gulch in the 1870s. Water was fed into iron pipes and hoses. High pressure torrents of water were sprayed out to erode entire hillsides into sluice boxes and rockers. By 1890, Virginia City was down to 600 residents. Another episode of mining occurred during the teens, as gold dredges tore up creek bottom gravels across the region. Huge piles of dredged placer diggings still extend for miles along Alder Creek. In the end, more than $100 million in gold was taken from this lucrative mining district.

During the 1940s, Charlie and Sue Bovey of Great Falls began to buy and stabilize buildings throughout Virginia City. Many structures had already been lost to firewood gatherers. Their efforts led to the designation of the town as a National Historic District in the 1970s.

The G. Goldberg Store (McGovern Dry Goods) is a wonderful wooden building erected in 1863. It is a Classic Greek Revival-style storefront with French doors. Between 1908 and 1945, Hanna and Mary McGovern operated a women's clothing store here. The inside is unchanged since their last day of business, including carefully laid out dresses, bolts of cloth, and sewing supplies. Betty Wright from Cape Code has a look inside.

Virginia City's mining-era history and role as Territorial Capitol (1865 through 1875) make it unique in the state. The downtown is a living architectural gallery containing forty-five historic commercial structures, thirty-two of which date from the 1860s and 1870s boomtown period. Round log, hewn log, wood-sided, stone, brick, and wood frame structures line Main Street in Gothic Revival, Classical Revival, Italianate, and vernacular styles. The Montana Post

The Kiskadden's Store Block (1863) was Virginia City's first stone building and once contained three stores downstairs and a meeting hall upstairs. The vigilantes would gather here to plan their raids on suspected road agents. Locals call this the "Vigilante Barn."

Building (1864) has a storefront of board-and-batten design with arched gothic windows. Content Corner (1864) still houses a restaurant/bar and general store. The Opera House (1900) is a rubble stone barn that now serves as the home of the Virginia City Players. During the summer, nightly melodramas are staged here. The Sauerbier Blacksmith Shop contains original tools hung on the walls. The brick Madison County Courthouse (1875) continues to house local government offices. Be sure to have a meal at the converted Wells Fargo building. The Fairweather Inn offers rustic overnight accommodations with a bathroom down the hall.

Virginia City is an elderly town by Montana standards. It has the oldest continuously-published newspaper in the state. The *Madisonian* has been issued every week since 13 November 1871. Yet, this is a town whose history has not been allowed to dissolve. Virginia City's tourist economy is fully dependent on historic preservation. Unlike Bannack (see page 85), which did not survive when the gold played out, Virginia City is still a vibrant living place with about 150 year-round residents.

The appalling violence of the Plummer Gang and the merciless retribution of the Virginia City vigilantes has now been reprieved to the quaintness of the past. In 1997, the State of Montana purchased Virginia and Nevada cities, ensuring their preservation.

OF RELATED INTEREST:
Hard Places: Reading the Landscape of America's Historic Mining Districts, by Richard V. Francaviglia (1991).

Little Bighorn
Battlefield

THE LITTLE BIGHORN BATTLEFIELD National Monument is a landscape of windswept sweetgrass and quiet coulees meandering past sandstone bluffs. The site of "Custer's Last Stand" is fifty-four miles southeast of Billings beside Interstate 90 within the Crow Reservation. The Visitors Center contains interpretive displays, artifacts such as the uniform of Colonel George Armstrong Custer, Indian weapons, and numerous photographs.

Just uphill is the final battle site. A stone monument over a mass grave and gravestones surrounded by an iron-rail fence mark the location of the "Last Stand." The Custer National Cemetery is downslope. Inside are the remains of soldiers, scouts, civilians, and Indians dating from the frontier era through the Vietnam War.

Opposite top:
Little Bighorn Battlefield.
The marble gravestones
were erected where soldiers
fell. The Visitors Center and
Custer National Cemetery
lay below.

Opposite below:
Re-enactment of the battle.
Photograph courtesy of the
Montana Department of
Commerce: Travel Montana

This landscape rests at the center of the Crow Nation—the "people of the Raven." The Little Bighorn Casino is operated by the Crow people within sight of the monument. Nearby is the new Indian Health Services building and the Ammaallsshuuwuua Crow Laundromat. In August, the Crow Indian Rodeo is held. This is the largest Indian rodeo in the country. Up to 5,000 tipis are erected along the Little Bighorn River.

Above all else, the Little Bighorn is a place where myths are buried but do not rest.

After the Civil War, the United States Army returned its attention to solving the West's "Indian Problem." The 1870s became a decade of great losses on both sides. The fragile American policy of treaty-making collapsed as waves of miners sought gold, and settlers drove stakes into the prairie. In direct violation of treaties with the Sioux, wagontrains full of emigrants entered the Black Hills gold fields. Colonel George Armstrong Custer, a Civil War hero, fought Sioux bands who defended their sacred mountain range. The Sioux called this bold man "Yellowhair."

In response to continued raiding by the Sioux and Cheyenne nations, U.S. commanders planned a three-pronged counterattack in the Little Bighorn country. George Armstrong Custer's Seventh Cavalry would

Custer's gravestone at the Little Bighorn. His body was removed from the battleground in 1877 and reinterred at West Point, New York. Photograph courtesy of the Montana Department of Commerce: Travel Montana.

outflank the Indians and attack from the south. Two separate forces of slower-moving infantry and cavalry would march from the Yellowstone River and strike from the north. The forces were to converge on the "renegades" and "rub them out."

On 25 June 1876, Custer's forces came upon an immense Indian encampment strung along several miles of the Little Bighorn River. It is estimated that 15,000 Sioux and Cheyenne, including thousands of braves, set up temporary residence along what they called the "Greasy Grass." Whether driven by blind foolishness, military pride, or political aspiration, Custer ignored the warnings of his officers and Crow scouts. He chose to attack immediately rather than wait for other forces to arrive.

Custer, Captain Frederick Benteen, and Major Marcus Reno each gathered about 200 men and fanned out to surround and punish the Indians. The forces of Benteen and Reno immediately suffered heavy casualties, pulled back, and dug in along a series of bluffs to the south near Medicine Tail Coulee. Custer was

unaware of these losses and arrogantly charged toward
the riverside encampment from the east. The great
chiefs, Gall and Crazy Horse, swept in with uncounted
numbers of warriors firing Winchester repeating rifles.
Custer and his men fought a ferocious, doomed retreat
along Battle Ridge to Custer Hill where they made a
"Last Stand" against the advancing wave of Indians.

Thirty minutes after his frontal assault began,
Custer and every one of his 209 men were killed. Reno
and Benteen fought on for another day until the
Indians broke camp rather than fight the approaching
columns of Army reinforcements. A total of 261
soldiers died in the Battle of the Little Bighorn. Only a
handful of Indians were killed.

The Sioux and Cheyenne claimed a complete but
pyrrhic victory. Press reports of the "Custer Massacre"
portrayed the Indians as blood-thirsty savages. The
public screamed for revenge. Federal efforts to "tame"
the Indians were increased, and soon all Western tribes
were corralled on reservations.

Until 1994, the Little Bighorn Battlefield National
Monument was called the "Custer Battlefield." Today,
Custer is no longer the only focus of this event. The
battlefield is now a place of remembrance of the
Indians who fought here as well. As you stand at the
sandstone obelisk bearing the names of the fallen
Army soldiers, remember that this was neither a
massacre nor an unprovoked killing of a "valiant"
leader. This was war. The Sioux and Cheyenne were
defending their land and families against an invasion.
The tilted marble gravestones found scattered around
the battlefield are somber reminders of the loss of
young soldiers. But look out over the shifting colors of
the Great Plains and consider what the Indian people
lost after this battle. In 1891, more than 300 Indian
people were slaughtered by U.S. troops at Wounded
Knee, South Dakota. A free way of life on the Plains
was gone forever.

In the 1970s, coal development companies approached the Crow and Northern Cheyenne nations
with plans for expanding coal production on tribal
lands. The Crow, like the Navajo in Arizona and New

Mexico, have been receptive to this strip-mining. The Northern Cheyenne have allowed some extraction but have successfully petitioned the federal government to receive "Class I Air Status" for their reservation. This protects their air quality against future coal-fired electrical generating plants.

The Crow and Northern Cheyenne tribes now live on adjacent reservations. The two nations generally get along well except when it comes to basketball games between the high schools of Lodgegrass (population 517) and Lame Deer (population 635). However, the relative sizes of their reservations are instructive. The Crow served as Custer's scouts and have a reservation containing 2,295,092 acres. The Northern Cheyenne fought Custer and received only 445,000 acres.

THE WHOLE STORY: *Bury My Heart At Wounded Knee,* by Dee Brown (1970), and *Son of the Morning Star,* by Evan S. Connell (1984).

Kootenai Falls

HALFWAY BETWEEN Libby and Troy in extreme northwest Montana, the Kootenai River has carved one this country's most awesome natural features— Kootenai Falls. If you can, park and walk the quarter mile to an overlook. Prepare to be humbled.

In this narrow cataract and falls, the Kootenai River drops more than 200 feet in a short distance. Stand back from the roar. Falling in the river is inadvisable for the living.

The falls and plunging rapids occur within a "narrows" at the bottom of a steep-sided canyon. The bedrock here, like in Glacier National Park, is composed of Precambrian mudstones and quartzites formed when much of Montana was covered by a vast, shallow inland sea. This is billion-year-old basement rock—the bottom of the stratigraphic profile.

Opposite:
Kootenai Falls is Montana's Niagara. The main falls (left center) were used in the movie "The River Wild" (1994) and called "The Gauntlet." Trick photography was used. Neither Actress Meryl Streep nor anyone but the most skillful and crazed river rats could row a raft through this falls and survive. Photograph by Philip Maechling.

Until about 15,000 years ago, this valley was filled by massive glaciers. Since the melting of the ice sheets, the intensely powerful Kootenai River has scoured and cut its channel deeper and deeper into the Earth's solid crust.

Indians have travelled through this canyon for at least 8,000 years. An Indian trail on the north bank of the river leads to many "vision quest sites." Artifacts such as spear points, arrowheads, knives, scrappers, jewelry, and fishing net sinkers carved in black obsidian, green argillite, and a rainbow of chert rocks have been found here by archaeologists. Stone effigy figures covered with red ochre have been unearthed but not deciphered.

Places such as Kootenai Falls are seen in strongly opposing ways. Engineers have repeatedly proposed that a hydroelectric dam be built here to harness the river's natural power. The Kootenai Indians view the Falls as a sacred source of knowledge, visions, and medicine: The dwelling place of guardian spirits they call "nupikas." Conservationists revere the place as a scenic and ecological treasure. Thus far, at least, dams have been kept from destroying this awesome natural and spiritual resource.

OF USE HERE AND ELSEWHERE:
Roadside Geology of Montana, by David Alt and Donald W. Hyndman (1992).

Flathead Indian Reservation

WESTERN MONTANA'S Flathead Indian Reservation is a landscape that eludes our expectations.

In 1855, a meeting was held near Missoula between various Indian nations and Washington Territorial Governor Isaac Stevens (Montana Territory wasn't created until 1864). Beside the Clark Fork River at a cottonwood forest known as Council Grove, it was agreed that the Salish, Kootenai, and Pend d'Oreille tribes would receive a large reservation extending north from Arlee near the Jocko River to Flathead Lake. Chief Victor's Flathead (Salish) band refused to leave the Bitterroot Valley. Charlot (Victor's son) resisted until 1891 when hunger, isolation, and a forged signature of the Chief on a treaty led to the bands' final exit from what trappers had called "the Salish Land."

The Indian nations co-existed well on the Reservation. Horses and bison were allowed to roam free. Hunting, fishing, and collecting wild onions, camas, bitterroots, huckleberries, and serviceberries provided ties to traditional ways of life that government flour, beans, and beef could not. Wild plants provided spiritual and physical medicine.

Today, the Flathead Reservation is highly Catholic. The tribes openly accepted the Jesuit priest, Father Pierre DeSmet, in 1854. In 1880, a school for boys was built, and, a decade later, the Ursuline nuns opened a nursery school. In 1891, the large and impressive St. Ignatius Mission was completed. It is still a main center of church life on the Reservation.

The Flathead Reservation is home to members of the Confederation Salish and Kootenai tribes, yet the majority of residents are white people. An 1887 piece of legislation known as the Dawes Act required tribes to do away with common ownership of land in reservations. Each head of a household was forced to choose a 160-acre parcel (the same acreage in the original Homestead Act of 1862) or to have the Indian Agent decide for them. These allotments could not be sold for twenty-five years. The government then opened unalloted land to homesteading by whites.

The south shore of Flathead Lake and Reservation farmland.

The St. Ignatius Mission was completed in 1891. This fine brick church has a bell tower 100 feet high. Inside are incredibly beautiful biblical murals painted on the ceiling by Joseph Carignano, the mission cook. Carignano had no formal art training. The ceiling murals at St. Francis Xavier church in Missoula were also painted by this soulful man.

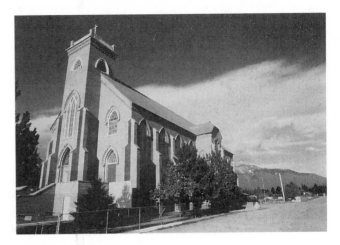

A bison roundup on the National Bison Range. A white bison called "Big Medicine" by the Flathead Indians was born here in 1933. Until his death in 1959, this biologically rare animal was a source of great spiritual meaning to local tribes. Photograph courtesy of the Montana Department of Commerce: Travel Montana.

By the time the law was overturned in 1912, about half of the 1,242,969-acre Flathead Reservation had fallen into non-tribal hands. Most of the prosperous ranches and farms in the Mission Valley were created in this way. Housing and commercial developments now cover former tribal lands. In 1997, the National Trust for Historic Preservation listed the Flathead Reservation as one of "America's Eleven Most Endangered Historic Places."

The National Bison Range is located at Moiese, about thirty-eight miles north of Missoula on Highway 212. This 18,500-acre reserve was formed in 1908 as habitat for the then endangered American bison.

Today, nearly 500 bison and many elk, deer, antelope, and golden eagles grace the landscape. Wildlife can be observed along a nineteen-mile dirt road that loops through the sanctuary.

About half of Flathead Lake is included in the Reservation. This is the largest freshwater lake west of the Mississippi River. It is twenty-eight miles long, eight to fifteen miles wide, with 185 miles of shoreline. Maximum depths reach 370 feet. Originally formed as part of Glacial Lake Missoula during the Ice Age, the lake is now impounded by Kerr Dam near Polson (elevation 2,917 feet; population 3,283). The fishery is dominated by rainbow, lake, and brown trout with decreasing numbers of Kokanee salmon. Sewage effluent and agricultural runoff are responsible for the lake's declining water quality. Recreational homes line the water's edge.

Driving north through the Reservation on Highway 93, you pass through the small towns of Arlee, Ravalli, St. Ignatius, Ronan, and Pablo. The Ninepipes and Pablo national wildlife refuges are a mosaic of glacial pothole lakes (kettles) that provide vital habitat for waterfowl. In the settlements, Reservation housing conditions reveal that poverty remains all too common here. Alcoholism affects far too many families. One of the main Reservation businesses is Doug Allard's Trading Post at St. Ignatius. Blankets, artwork, bead necklaces, and other goods are available for purchase. Be sure to look for the work of local Indian artists; much of what you see comes from Arizona and New Mexico.

OF RELATED INTEREST: *Irredeemable America: The Indian's Estate and Land Claims,* Edited by Imre Sutton (1985), and the poetry of Richard Hugo, including *The Lady at Kicking Horse Reservoir* (1972) and *Making Certain It Goes On: The Collected Poems of Richard Hugo* (1984).

Rising above the Reservation are the 10,000-foot peaks of the Mission Range. These fault-block mountains were carved by glaciers into some of Montana's most elegant topography. Small glaciers still exist in the high country. Grizzly bears range across the alpine meadows. The face of the mountains is part of the sacred Mission Mountains Tribal Wilderness, the only Indian Wilderness in the United States. It is off-limits to non-tribal members. Tribal recreation permits are required for visits to portions of the Reservation that are open to the public.

The Rocky Mountain
Front

THE ROCKY MOUNTAIN FRONT is a windy
landscape of powerful contrasts. It is a place where the
Great Plains and the Rocky Mountains converge to
form one of Montana's most spectacular terrains. This
handsome, spacious expanse extends south from the
Canadian border to the Missouri River.

The mountains are composed of slightly folded
limestones and sandstones. Much of the high country
is included in what geologists call the "Overthrust
Belt." Entire mountain ranges have been thrust
eastward along low-angle faults into their present

The author in Glacier
National Park in 1975.
Photograph by Betty Wright.

positions. Oil deposits exist here, and there are on-
going conflicts over petroleum exploration in wilderness areas. The plains are underlain by flat-lying
sedimentary rocks unaffected by nearby mountain-
building events. However, several large, flat-topped
buttes stand above the countryside. Crown and Square
buttes (west of Great Falls) are capped by a dark
igneous rock called shonkonite. Fifty million years
ago, molten magma with a composition much like
basalt was intruded between beds of sedimentary
rocks. This magma hardened into bubbles called
laccoliths. Erosion has worn away the surrounding soft
rocks. The highly resistant shonkonite layers form the
tops of the buttes.

During the Ice Age, vast continental glaciers moved
from Canada as far south in Montana as the present
course of the Missouri River. Mountain glaciers
extended out from canyons along the Rocky Mountain
Front. Glacial Lake Great Falls was created as the ice
sheets melted. Blocks of ice were scattered across the
landscape and encased in sediments. As the "bergs"
slowly melted, pothole lakes formed all along the
Front. These lakes are most abundant between Browning and Dupuyer.

The Marias, Teton, Sun, and Dearborn rivers and
dozens of smaller streams drain eastward from the
mountains. Spectacular canyons have been carved in
many watersheds. The abundance of water and rich
soils led to nineteenth-century homesteading and the
formation of towns such as Valier, Dupuyer, and
Choteau. "The Front" was first occupied, however, by
a succession of Indian tribes and migrants along the
Old North Trail.

During the early 1800s, the Blackfeet (Sikiska),
Blood, and Piegan nations comprised the Blackfoot
Confederacy. This powerful alliance controlled the fur
trade along the Front and throughout much of the
Northern Plains. Raiding parties traveled as far south
as Mexico in search of ponies and other wealth. In
1851, Congress created the 1,525,712-acre Blackfeet
Indian Reservation east of present-day Glacier National Park as a home for the three tribes. The Holy

The Rocky Mountain Front, an astonishing landscape from peaks to prairies. Photograph courtesy of The Nature Conservancy, Big Sky Field Office, Helena

Family Mission was built in Browning by Catholic priests. Browning's Museum of the Plains Indian contains displays conveying the complex cultures and creative artistry of American Indians.

The Rocky Mountain Front is one of America's most ecologically intact landscapes. Grizzly bears, gray wolves, elk, deer, bighorn sheep, bald and golden eagles, countless waterbirds, trout, and scores of other creatures rely on the prairies, rivers, wetlands, and forests of the Front. There is an on-going effort to conserve the region from development. The federal government has created the Scapegoat, Bob Marshall, and Great Bear wilderness areas (1,534,993 acres), as well as Glacier National Park (1,013,000 acres). The state has established numerous conservation lands, including the Blackleaf, Sun River, Willow Creek, Pishkun Reservoir, Freezeout Lake, and Ear Mountain wildlife management areas. Land trust groups such as The Nature Conservancy, The Conservation Fund, and the Montana Land Reliance have worked for years with landowners to protect key private lands from subdivision and housing development.

The Nature Conservancy's Pine Butte Swamp Preserve, located twelve miles west of Choteau, is one of America's finest. This 18,000-acre expanse is one of the last places in the lower forty-eight states where grizzly bears roam their original Great Plains habitat. The preserve is home to forty-three species of mammals, 185 species of birds, and a stunning array of plant life. It has a guest ranch and natural history center.

Included in the Pine Butte Swamp Preserve is a small hill with the grand name of "Egg Mountain." In the 1980s, scientists unearthed the bones of scores of duck-billed dinosaurs on the Peebles Ranch. A volcanic eruption about 100 million years ago

A sow grizzly bear and cub at The Nature Conservancy's Pine Butte Swamp Preserve. Photograph courtesy of The Nature Conservancy, Big Sky Field Office, Helena.

entombed nests full of eggs and many baby dinosaurs about the size of large house cats. This new find was named Maiasaura, which means "good mother dinosaur." On-site evidence reveals that the eggs were guarded, and the young were carefully fed and tended —much like modern birds.

The open vistas and ample solitude of the Rocky Mountain Front are precious. You are visiting a landscape with a sense of eternity all around. This place is Montana's heartland. Tread lightly.

LITERARY ROOTS: *This House of Sky*, by Ivan Doig (1978), and *Digging Dinosaurs*, by John R. Horner (1988).

A 1935 photograph by Mable Mansfield of Bob Marshall, a cofounder of the Wilderness Society, during one of his many hiking treks to the wilds of Montana. "The Bob" was officially designated a national wilderness area in 1940 after Mr. Marshall's death in 1939. Photograph courtesy of The Wilderness Society, Washington, D.C.

Gates of the Mountains and Mann Gulch

ON 19 JULY 1805, the Lewis and Clark Expedition paddled south on the Missouri River above Great Falls. The party entered a deep canyon and struggled up a series of rapids. A tremendous hailstorm pounded their backs and splashed violently all around them.

Meriwether Lewis wrote: "These cliffs rise from the water's edge on either side perpendicularly to a height of 1,200 feet, every object here wears a dark and gloomy aspect, the towering rocks in many places seem ready to tumble on us, the river appears to have forced its way through this immense body of solid rock for a distance of 5-3/4 miles . . . from the singular appearance of this place I called it the gates of the rocky mountains." This spectacular canyon, lying twenty miles north of Helena, the state capital, still carries that name.

The Gates of the Mountains is best enjoyed by boat on Upper Holter Lake. Photograph courtesy of the U.S. Forest Service.

The steamboat, Rose of Helena, carried tourists through the scenic Gates of the Mountains between 1886 and 1906. In 1907, Holter Dam was built, and water backed up into the Gates creating Upper Holter Lake. This was the beginning of the "reclamation" period on the rivers of the American West. Many dams would follow on the Colorado, Green, Columbia, and other waterways. The resulting irrigation of farmland and generation of electricity for urban expansion would transform the region. With the Holter Dam, the Missouri was harnessed, but the landscape has remained wild.

The rugged bedrock walls of the Gates of the Mountains are composed of Mississippian-aged (300 million years old) Madison Limestone. These light gray to whitish rocks were formed in the clear, warm waters of a tropical sea much like today's Caribbean. The tightly folded strata and ledges of Madison Limestone are rich in fossil corals and the shells of invertebrates known as Brachiopods: Clams, mollusks, and mussels. Gold and silver deposits associated with the El Dorado overthrust fault were mined in the surrounding country. Placer gold mining occurred in the sand and gravel deposits known as the Ming Bar (named for Chinese laborers).

This region contains abundant elk, bighorn sheep, mountain goats, bald and golden eagles, falcons, and hawks. The Gates of the Mountains Wilderness, Gates of the Mountains Game Preserve, and Beartooth Wildlife Management Area encircle the canyon. Many waterfowl species use Upper Holter Lake as nesting or migratory habitat. The Missouri River is rated a "Class I" fishery resource. Osprey can often be seen scooping rainbow trout from the water. A boat dock exists on Upper Holter Lake where commercial boat trips up the canyon can be taken during the summer months.

Four miles downstream from Upper Holter Lake is Mann Gulch.

On 5 August 1949, a crew of fifteen elite "smoke-jumpers" parachuted into this steep box-canyon to fight a wildfire set off by lightning strikes. Conditions were scorching. Temperatures on the ground exceeded

A cross marks the spot where smokejumper Stanley J. Reba died in the 1959 Mann Gulch fire. Norman Maclean's book about the tragedy, *Young Men and Fire*, makes this site worthy of national literary landmark status. Photograph courtesy of the U.S. Forest Service.

NECESSARY READING:
Young Men and Fire,
by Norman Maclean (1992).

100 degrees Fahrenheit, and the forests were baked. Tinder-dry grasslands crunched underfoot. Powerful winds began to blow a wall of fire up the steep grassy slopes. The flames quickly exploded into a firestorm. The smokejumpers were trapped. The men raced upslope seeking safety over a ridgeline, but only two made it. Thirteen strong, confident firefighters died. Crosses mark the places where they fell.

The Mann Gulch fire led to the earliest reassessment of the nation's policy of fire suppression. Time has shown that fire is a natural part of the ecology of forests and grasslands. Burns release fertility and assure the continued health of ecosystems. Many are now questioning whether fires in remote, unpopulated areas can or should be put out. Mann Gulch is vital ground. It teaches us that fire is inevitable in the West. It reminds us that the cost of fighting that fact can be heartbreaking.

The High-Line   THE HIGH-LINE is a 440-mile long corridor of rolling
wheat lands and small farming towns scattered east-
west along Highway 2. This place demarcates the
northern Montana "high" plains. It is a cultural
landscape conceived in the mind of one man, railroad
magnate James J. Hill, "The Empire Builder." Although the High-Line is now a string of hinterland
agricultural communities, Hill once had grand plans
for the place.

In 1887, Hill completed the construction of the
Great Northern Railroad across Montana's mostly
unpopulated and semi-arid northern tier. "The Empire
Builder" now linked St. Paul, Minnesota, with Everett,
Washington, a tough stretch of country. Hill bragged,
"Give me enough Swedes and whiskey and I'll build a
railroad through Hell!" Few doubted him.

Hill had learned of a new system of dryland agriculture developed on the Canadian plains by a far-sighted
agronomist named Angus Mackay. This new approach
was called the "summer fallow system." Mackay's
fallow method involved plowing up the prairies,
planting one strip into wheat, and letting an adjacent
strip remain fallow for one year to accumulate soil
moisture. Even during drought years, yields in Canada
on fallowed soils averaged 35 bushels per acre; con-
tinuously cropped fields produced but two bushels per
acre.

Yet, this new way of farming caught on slowly until
1890 when a South Dakota farmer named Hardy
Webster Campbell published his "Soil Culture
Manual." James J. Hill now had a promotional angle
for luring settlers to the lands along his Great Northern
Railroad. Hill hired Campbell to sell the idea of dry
farming in the Northern Plains. Campbell responded
with vigor: "I believe that this region is destined to be
the last and best grain gardenry of the world."

Campbell's message led to the passage of the
Enlarged Homestead Act in 1909 and set off Montana's
most heartbreaking settlement period. This federal law
provided 320 acres free to anyone willing to move to
the Plains, work the land for three years to "prove it
up," and gain title. Land could also be bought directly

Strips of dryland wheat dominate much of the High-Line.

from the Great Northern Railroad which had been granted 13.5 million acres along its right-of-way by the federal government. Prices ranged from $1 to $8.56 per acre, a sizeable sum at the time. The company sold eleven million acres in eight years. Speculators sometimes bought up prime tracts and re-sold them for exorbitant prices.

The Great Northern sent rail car exhibits displaying the real and imagined bounty of the Plains across the country. A company poster showed a farmer turning over the sod and gold coins pouring out. Settlers from the Midwest and Europe believed it all and came in immense numbers.

A grain elevator complex in Glasgow.

An abandoned homestead is a common sight along the High-Line.

During the first three months of 1910, the Great
Northern rolled more than 1,000 rail cars full of
homesteaders into wheat boom towns. On one March
day, 250 settlers arrived at Havre, increasing the
population by one-third. The Great Northern offered
cheap one-way tickets. It cost only $22.50 for a family
of four plus their livestock to ride from St. Paul to the
High-Line. Heading back cost ten times that much.

At first, most homesteaders prospered. Rainfall
averaged sixteen inches per year from 1910 to 1916,
double the long-term norm. Yields rose from 11
million bushels in 1909 to more than 42 million
bushels in the "Miracle Year" of 1915. Prices for
Montana's superb, high protein spring and winter
wheat reached record levels during World War I.
Homesteaders took all this in stride: The promoters
had promised great things, and it all was coming true.
Due to the influx of settlers, the three High-Line
counties of 1910 had been split into fifteen counties by
1922. But most of the settlers still lived in 12-foot by
18-foot tarpaper shacks. Ranchers didn't care much for
these greenhorns and called them "honyockers"—a
derogatory German slang expression for "chicken
chaser."

In 1919, drought returned to the High-Line. Soil
dried to dust, and clouds of grasshoppers devoured
much of the meager crops. The end of World War I
caused wheat prices to plummet. Most High-Line
honyockers went bankrupt. The state's population had
skyrocketed from 243,329 in 1900 to an estimated
750,000 in 1918 because of the farming boom. This
remains the biggest growth period in Montana's
history. Yet, the end of the wheat boom caused the
state's population to plunge to 548,889 by 1920, a
record 29% decline. The High-Line exodus was even
more dramatic. By 1920, 65,000 of the 85,000 homesteaders had abandoned their farms and left the
region. Montana's wheat bonanza had collapsed.

Today, the High-Line is littered with abandoned
buildings. Yet, quiet wheat towns such as Glasgow,
Malta, Chinook, Havre, and Shelby have survived
beside Hill's tracks (now owned by the Burlington

Northern Railroad). Concrete grain elevators are the dominant landmarks. Most towns are arranged as strips along the tracks (for example, Dodson and Saco) or as a "T", with a linear strip and a main street forming the stem (Kremlin and Rudyard). The High-Line also has some of the best preserved early twentieth-century commercial architecture in America, among it Twedt's Garage in Rudyard, Barnard's gas station in Saco, and many old tourist courts and cabins along the roadway.

Today, High-Line life is plain and realistic. Most farms are more than 4,000 acres in size, having been pieced together from old 320-acre homesteads. One operation near Chester is called the "97 Homesteads" farm. The landscape is tidy, geometrical, and modestly productive. Strips of wheat and fallow land alternate in an endless, repeating pattern. Nearly all the plowing is done north-south to reduce the erosive effect of the prevailing westerly winds. Irrigated agriculture is only practiced near impoundments such as the Tiber Reservoir south of Galata.

HIGHLY RECOMMENDED:
Plains Country Towns,
by John C. Hudson (1986), and
Great Plains, by Ian Frazier
(1989).

The High-Line never matched the grand dimensions of Mr. Hill's dream. Aridity imposed its limits, and painful lessons were learned. What has remained is an efficiently beautiful region built on that hard-won knowledge of land and life.

Hutterite Colonies

THE LANDSCAPE of Central Montana is defined by its abundant isolation. The region has always attracted dreamers wishing to transform a chaotic big world into small portions of utopia.

Across the Judith Basin, the High-Line, and the Rocky Mountain Front are more than forty tidy, orderly groups of houses, barns, and granaries. These are the farming "Colonies" of an Anabaptist religious group known as the Hutterites.

The origins of this religious sect extend back to early sixteenth-century South Germany and Austria. The radical Protestant Reformation fractured

The tidy architecture of a Hutterite colony. Never enter without first gaining permission from an "Elder."

"Christendom" into many sects. One group of Moravian Anabaptists was led by Jakob Hutter, who was not a highly-educated man but one possessed of unique leadership ability. The Hutterite, Mennonite, and Swiss Brethren Anabaptists believed that religious practice should be free from the intervention of a Pope or any other grand leader. Infant baptism was rejected in favor of Anabaptism, the baptizing of adults who had freely found their way to God. The Mennonites, Hutterites, and Swiss Brethren (primarily the Amish) farmed in quiet corners of Europe before emigrating to North America beginning in 1683 in search of greater freedom. Most Anabaptists initially settled in Pennsylvania, near Lancaster, during the eighteen century, and many remain today.

Hutterites arrived in Montana in the 1880s. Communal farming colonies were established outside small towns such as Harlowton, Judith Gap, Stanford, Lewistown, and Conrad. Other colonies were established in the Alberta plains of Canada and in the Dakotas. Wheat, oats, barley, and cattle were raised. Land stewardship, faith in God, and the company of colony members formed the foundation of life. This is still true today.

Hutterite colonies wear a distinctive look. Wide-frame, two-story houses with gable roofs stand at precise distances from each other. Most contain the residences of several families. Picket fences, sheds, and outbuildings are carefully tended. Most colonies are prosperous, and extra money is spent on equipment. Hutterites shun most aspects of modern life, yet they use up-to-date farm machinery and drive pickup trucks. Children are primarily educated in Colony schools and maintain the group's German dialect. Like the Old Order Amish and Old Order Mennonites, Hutterite clothing is homemade and "plain." Women and girls wear long "prairie" dresses and sun bonnets. Married men have beards and don simple pants and work shirts. Although contact with outsiders is not sought, colonists are wary but generally polite to strangers. Relations with adjacent non-Hutterite families are wary but usually just fine.

In a land where farming is the chosen way of life, Hutterites invite respect. They are often given the high praise of being called "good ag managers." Most colony children grow up winning drawers full of ribbons at 4-H gatherings and county fairs.

The Hutterites came to North America in search of an agrarian utopia. On a sunny day etched with meadowlark songs, it is possible to look out over a colony and believe they have found it.

TO LEARN MORE:
Hutterite Society,
by John A. Hostetler (1974),
and *Religions of Montana,
Volume II,*
by Lawrence F. Small (1995).

Harlowton   HARLOWTON IS MONTANA'S classic railroad town.
It was platted ninety-two miles northwest of Billings
in an age of promise and flourished in an era of growth.
Today, a shiny Milwaukee Road locomotive stands at
the entrance to Central Avenue, but the rails have been
pulled up and the line abandoned.

The pattern of Eastern Montana's cultural landscape
was created by railroad companies. James J. Hill's and
J.P. Morgan's Great Northern and Northern Pacific
lines formed two east-west corridors across Montana
in the northern and southern portions of the state. The
adjacent landscapes were opened to farming and
ranching. The rich grasslands along Central Montana's
Musselshell River also had great potential for homesteading and formed a natural third traverse across
Montana toward the Pacific Ocean.

In 1906, The Chicago, Milwaukee & St. Paul and
Pacific Railway Company (commonly known as the
Milwaukee Road) acquired right-of-way and began
laying track across Central Montana. Hill and Morgan
attempted to block this competing line.

Richard Harlow's small Central Montana Railway
lay on the Milwaukee Road's proposed route. Harlow's
unprofitable outfit provided connecting rail service
between Hill's and Morgan's major east-west lines. It
was known as the "Jawbone Railroad," named after
Harlow's tendency to make big promises instead of
paying his bills. He platted a community beside the
Musselshell River which he immodestly called
Harlowton. The Milwaukee Road purchased the
Jawbone and reached Harlowton in 1908. The route
then proceeded to Butte and down the Clark Fork
Valley to Idaho. By 1909, the Enlarged Homestead Act
was luring thousands of homesteading "honyockers"
into the Musselshell and Judith basins. Most arrived by
rail: In seven years, more than 28,000 walked off
crowded railcars into Harlowton. After World War I,
drought and falling wheat prices forced most to leave
the area.

The Milwaukee Road had incurred huge debts in
constructing its line, and the company was now out-

The faded elegance of the Graves Hotel in Harlowton.

competed by Hill and Morgan. In a bold move, the Milwaukee Road electrified 438 miles of the line extending from Harlowton west to Idaho. This became the longest electrified line in the United States. Power lines paralleled the tracks, and huge brick transformer stations were built every thirty miles. The transformers converted 100,000 volts of A.C. from the electrical lines into 3,000 volts of D.C. This power was then picked up by the train through copper wires hung above the tracks. The engines were designed to save energy by the use of "regenerative braking systems." This converted the brakes to electrical generators on downhill stretches. About half the power used to ascend a steep grade was regenerated on the frequent steep descents. Yet, even this proved insufficient to make the line operate profitably, and the Milwaukee Road fell into receivership in 1925. It was soon revived, and, for many years, Harlowton served as a Division Point and home for many railroad employees.

In the late-1970s, the Milwaukee Road once again declared bankruptcy, and the road bed was stripped of rails and sold. Abandoned transformer stations can be seen all along the former Milwaukee right-of-way. Harlowton lost scores of jobs and has continued to decline.

Opposite: **The abandoned Milwaukee Road railway depot in Harlowton. One small engine and thirty feet of track are all that remain of the railroad boom.**

The community, however, remains a pleasant farming town with a population of 1,049. It is the county seat of Wheatland County (population 2,246). Life is straightforward and functional. A museum of the railroading days is found in the Times Block. The most prominent building in town is the three-story Graves Hotel (1908) located atop Central Avenue Hill. This once-grand railroad hotel was built in a Gothic Revival style using sandstone cut from nearby bluffs. Its wooden cornices and metal cupola are reminders of Harlowton's days of optimism, when well-dressed farmers danced to thirty-piece orchestras. The hotel and restaurant are often closed these days. Sit on the porch or the second-story veranda and look south to the abandoned depot and roundhouses. In the past, steam engines were used to pull all trains east of Harlowton on the Milwaukee Road. Electrical locomo-

OF RELATED INTEREST: *The Story of the Western Railroads,* by Robert E. Riegel (1926).

tives were once used west of this division point. The quiet reveals that the railroad is now gone for good.

The survival of Harlowton shows the will of rural Montanans to stick it out in tough places they choose to call home.

Fort Peck Dam and Reservoir

FORT PECK RESERVOIR is the place where the New Deal came to Big Sky Country. It is the site of the largest and oldest earth-filled dam in the world—Montana's Pyramid of Giza.

The Depression of the 1930s threatened to crush the spirit of America. President Franklin Delano Roosevelt instructed the Works Progress Administration and the U.S. Army Corps of Engineers to begin an ambitious dam building project on the Missouri River. The stated rationale for the massive earth-filled dam was to control flooding, generate electricity, and improve river navigation. The real reason was to make jobs.

At the peak of construction in 1936, 10,500 Depression-bled workers were hired to plug the Missouri River. A trestle spanned the site, and railroad cars dumped countless loads of fill into the valley bottom. The government built a centrally planned town called Fort Peck complete with a 1,600-seat movie theater. Shantytown camps and boomtowns, however, with names such as "New Deal," "Square Deal," and "Wheeler," housed most workers. The "Happy Hollow" red light district and Ruby Smith's Bar were popular hang-outs. When FDR visited the construction site in 1937, he was carefully guided away from these local attractions.

The Fort Peck Dam closed off the Missouri River in 1937 and was completed in 1940. The cost of the project was $110 million. Everything about this feature is immense. The dam is four miles long, 3,500 feet thick at its base, and 250 feet high. Its concrete-lined spillway is one mile long with a capacity of

The Fort Peck Dam and Reservoir. The main embankment contains 126 million cubic yards of earth: Enough to cover a football field with a pile of dirt 2-1/2 miles high. Fishing is a popular activity in the reservoir. Photograph courtesy of the U.S. Army Corps of Engineers.

ALL THE FACTS: *Fort Peck: A Half-century and Holding,* by U.S. Army Corps of Engineers (1987).

250,000 cubic feet per second of flow (1.9 million gallons each second). The hydroelectric plant can generate 185,000 kilowatts of power. The Fort Peck Reservoir extends for 175 miles east-west, has 1,900 miles of deeply embayed shoreline, covers 245,000 acres, and holds more than 20 million acre feet of water (6.5 trillion gallons). Recreation sites and boat docks are scattered around the edge of the water.

The town of Fort Peck is now home to only 325 people. Most residents work for the U.S. Army Corps of Engineers, which operates the facility, or they provide services to the tourists. Fort Peck Reservoir has an excellent and diverse fishery noted for northern pike, walleye, lake trout, shovelnose sturgeon, sauger, burbot, paddlefish, and channel catfish. The rare pallid sturgeon is found here as well.

A fine collection of fossils entombed in slabs of the Bearpaw Shale is housed in the power plant museum. Fossilized dinosaur bones and eggs, armored fish, reptiles, palm trees, and figs can be seen. The only known bones of an Akylosaurus, a club-tailed, horned creature twenty-four feet long, are on display. The museum's photographs of the dam's construction are remarkable.

The federal government leveled most of the original buildings after the dam project was completed. The Fort Peck Theater survived and is listed on the National Register of Historic Places. This Swiss Chalet/Arts and Crafts-style structure is located on Missouri Avenue. Eleven of the original permanent residence homes can be seen on what workers called "Big Shots Row" (1100-1112 East Kansas Avenue). Most of the other buildings in town were built after 1960.

In the 1930s, critics of the Fort Peck project called it "Roosevelt's Duck Pond." Although the dam has not ended flooding on the Missouri River nor has it aided navigation in any measurable way, it helped bail Montana out of the depths of the Depression. For that and the abundant habitat it provides in the Charles M. Russell National Wildlife Refuge, we can be grateful.

The Fort Peck Theater being repainted as the home of popular summer theatrical productions.

Miles City   MILES CITY is Montana's purest cowtown. This pleasant community of 8,461 is located beside the Yellowstone River where the Tongue River adds its muddy water. The Indians called this widely meandering tributary the Tongue because "it is like the White Man's tongue, crooked."

Lewis and Clark and countless fur trappers passed here on the "Roche Jaune Rivière" (Yellowstone River). Yet, Miles City was not established until 1877 when Fort Keogh was built following the Sioux/ Northern Cheyenne War. The town was named for the garrison's commander, Colonel Nelson A. Miles, the man who accepted the surrender of Chief Joseph's Nez Perce band near the Canadian border.

Miles City quickly became the dominant cowtown in the Montana Territory. The 1880s was the era of the "Open Range" where calves were branded in the spring, turned loose for a year on the plains, and rounded up for sale. A rider could travel for days across Eastern Montana without encountering a barbed wire fence.

The Northern Pacific Railroad reached Miles City in 1881. Cattle herds were trailed-in by the hundreds from as far away as Texas to be shipped "Back East." The city railyard was a high-smelling warren of holding corrals, chutes, and loading docks filled with bawling cows. Downtown was a clutter of saloons, boarding houses, liveries, bordellos, and banks. Cowboys, clerks, and cavalrymen managed to keep things stirred up.

The cowboy is America's most enduring myth. Portrayed as Galahads of the Plains, most were uneducated migrant laborers who worked in horrible conditions for a few dollars a month. Whether white, black, hispanic, or of mixed ancestry, the job of a cowboy was to drive herds of manure-stained, semi-feral cattle through rain, hail, mud, dust, and sun for weeks at a time. Their grub was just as monotonous: Mostly beef, bacon (or salt pork), beans, and bread. Trail coffee was not cappuccino but was an acrid, powerful beverage called the "Buckaroo's Brew." Some "Cookies" claimed their concoctions could "float a hoss-shoe."

Main Street in Miles City has plenty of watering holes.

It was no wonder that cowboys arriving in Miles City were primed to "let'r rip." Pay was quickly spent on whiskey and certain women at the Gray Mule Saloon. Rowdiness was the order of the day, but crimes were mostly barfights, petty theft, and gunplay. Despite the myths, most cowboys were neither heroic nor big trouble.

Miles City was a boomtown during the cattle bonanza of 1880 to 1886. In 1880, there were only 275,000 cattle in the entire Montana Territory. The destruction of bison herds and rising beef prices caused speculators to severely overstock the Plains. Without fencing to hold in the cattle, rustlers made off with

The Range Riders Museum, just outside Miles City, is the
guardian of a past that local ranchers refuse to let die.

tens of thousands of head. Despite the thievery, by
1883, the Territory had 600,000 cattle, with most of
these in Central and Eastern Montana. The short-grass
landscape began to show the strain.

In January of 1885, temperatures reached 52 degrees
below zero Fahrenheit at Miles City. Cattle came in off
the depleted range and wandered the streets looking for
food. During the scorching summer of 1886, grasses
withered, and enormous range fires turned the night
sky red for months. Water holes dried up. Creeks
turned to alkali pools. Cows began to die. In the fall, icy
gales swept in covering the sparse grasses with a thick
crust that lacerated the noses of cattle seeking forage.

In January of 1887, a month the Cheyenne call "the Moon of Cold-Exploding Trees," temperatures plunged to between 20 and 40 below and stayed there. Snow began to form deep drifts. A great blizzard hit Miles City. It got even colder—down to 63 below. Snow was now belly deep on a horse. Cattle wandered aimlessly, snowblind and desperate, their skin covered with sores and streaks of frozen blood. Many sought shelter in ravines where they slowly froze to death.

In the spring, the enormity of the losses became clear. A chinook (a warming wind that descends from the Rocky Mountains) finally came, and cowboys discovered a horrifying scene. For miles, the landscape was covered with the rotting carcasses of cattle. In places, the coulees were completely filled with bodies. During that catastrophic winter, 60% of the cattle in the Territory died: 362,000 head. Losses around Miles City were 95%. Almost half the cattle outfits in Custer County went bankrupt.

The tragic winter of 1886 to 1887 had shown the limits of the land. The days of the Open Range were over. Ranchers began to fence in the rangelands, provide cattle with winter feed, and develop water sources. Modern ranching in Montana was born.

The Range Riders Museum on Main Street just west of downtown Miles City is one of the state's best. It evokes the ranching life that grew up after the 1887 die-off. Inside are saddles, chaps, rifles, and fascinating frontier artifacts. A remarkable collection of more than 600 photographs of pioneer ranchers graces the walls of a large meeting hall.

Today, cowboying and the cattle business are far from dead. The stockyards of the Miles City Livestock Commission are nearby on Main Street. These yards were the end point of the Great American Cattle Drive of 1995. Hundreds of head were driven by cowboys on horseback from Houston, Texas, to Miles City over a four-month period. Like a scene from a century before, the herd was driven right through town past the Range Riders Bar and the Miles City Saddlery store.

WELL WORTH A LOOK: *Charles M. Russell: The Artist in His Heyday* (1995), and the Charles M. Russell Museum in Great Falls, Montana.

***Fort Union
Trading Post***

FUR PELTS WERE the first natural resource to be commercially exploited in Montana. Meriwether Lewis had recommended the confluence of the Yellowstone and Missouri rivers as a "most eligible site" for a fur trading post. In 1829, John Jacob Astor built Fort Union here on the north bank of the Missouri. This strategic location allowed the American Fur Company to dominate the highly profitable Montana fur trade for thirty years.

The cooperation of American Indians was essential for the original post to succeed. In the late 1820s, the Blackfoot Confederacy (Blackfeet, Piegans, and Bloods) controlled the fur trade in northern Montana, the beaver-rich Three Forks region, and southern Alberta in Canada. At first, Fort Union had to draw its furs from such tribes as the Crow and Assiniboine and from white "free trappers."

John Jacob Astor's American Fur Company soon dominated the fur trade. The company was well financed and used large steamboats instead of crude

Fort Union reconstructed.

Bourgeois House and Museum with the "AFC" (American Fur Company) flag flying over it.

keelboats to move furs quickly to St. Louis markets. The first steamboat, a stout craft called the Yellowstone, arrived in 1832.

Fort Union was one of the grandest trading posts in the West measuring 240 feet by 220 feet. It was surrounded by a palisade of hewn cottonwood pickets twenty feet high and one foot thick. Stone bastion houses, twenty-three feet wide and thirty feet high, were erected on the southwest and northeast corners and capped by pyramidal roofs. An impressive double-doored gate guarded the entrance. Inside were stone houses, wooden barracks, work shops, stables, tents, cannon, and a magazine holding 50,000 pounds of black powder. At its peak, the fort was home to more than 100 people. No British trading post could compare. James Audubon stayed here in grand style during a "birding" trip.

In the late 1830s, a tall, striking man named Alexander Culbertson took over operation of Fort Union after Astor sold out. Through his honesty, Culbertson established good relations with the Blackfoot Confederacy and other tribes. The fact that his wife, Matawista Iksana, was a Blood Indian, cemented the trust and trade of the native Americans.

The fur trade peaked during the 1830s and 1840s. This was the short-lived era of mountain men rendezvous and regular intermarriage between trappers and Indian women. Their offspring, known disparagingly as "half-breeds," were rarely accepted into either white or Indian cultures.

By the 1850s, beaver populations began to plummet from over-killing. Bison pelts still poured in, but Fort Union no longer controlled the trade. The expanding steamboat traffic to numerous other Montana trading posts cut deeply into its business. In 1867, Fort Union was dismantled, and the site was abandoned.

FOR ALL THE DETAILS:
The American Fur Trade of the Far West, two volumes, by Hiram M. Chittenden (1986).

The Fort is now a National Historic Site located astride the Montana/North Dakota border twenty-seven miles east of Culbertson. A remarkably faithful reconstruction of the Fort can be toured. The fine museum inside the Bourgeois House contains history displays, trade goods, pistols, clothing, beads, pipes and Indian artifacts. The Missouri River has shifted its channel south of the original dock landing, leaving the fort high and dry. Yet, its geographic and historic importance will never be forgotten.

Bannack   BANNACK WAS MONTANA'S first major gold camp and first territorial capitol. Located twenty-two miles southwest of Dillon, this once thriving community is now a 198-acre ghost town and state park managed in a condition of "arrested decay." Visitors just call it beautiful. This remote treasure is a headstone for one episode in the West's continuing cycles of boom and bust.

The Meade Hotel (1875) is a hybrid Classical Revival/
Federal design, built of brick, cut stone, and rubble stone.
This wonderful building served as the courthouse of
Beaverhead County until 1881. It was then operated as a
hotel until the 1940s. On the front porch are Berkeley
geographers and friends. The author is seated at the left
beside the late Jim Parsons; standing (from right to left) are
Ted Oberlander, Betty Parsons, Allison Ekdale, and Dave
Larson. Photograph by Tom Eley.

In the summer of 1862, John White found good "color" in placer diggings along Grasshopper Creek in the Beaverhead River drainage. Even with the Civil War raging, word spread like a chain lightning. By fall, more than 500 miners, greenhorns, and speculators had descended on Bannack, a place named after a local Shoshoni Indian tribe.

Finding gold in placer "diggin's" required no particular skill, just the essentials: A pick, shovel, water, and raw determination. The first pilgrims to Bannack used pans or coffee pots to separate sand and gravel from the gold. Soon sluiceboxes and rockers were constructed. Water washed away the sediment and nuggets, flakes, and gold dust were left behind. Mercury was also applied to amalgamate the gold. The streams and gravel terraces were ransacked.

Buildings soon replaced canvas tents as hotels, saloons, hardware stores, liveries, homes, and bordellos were erected. Road agents descended on Bannack to relieve miners of their instant wealth. A gang of thieves arrived from Idaho led by a charismatic psychopath named Henry Plummer. Plummer's Gang caused a crime wave which he boldly used as the central plank of his own law and order campaign for Sheriff. The public was conned into electing him.

In a few months, Bannack's population grew to 3,000, and the best gold claims were quickly grabbed. Feverish prospectors spread out all over the watersheds of the upper Missouri and Yellowstone rivers. In the spring of 1863, two weary Bannack miners named Henry Edgar and Bill Fairweather paused at a small stream called Alder Gulch to pan for tobacco money. Their first handful of gravel yielded $2.40 worth of gold. They returned to Bannack, quickly got supplies, and raced back to pan more gold. To their dismay, Edgar and Fairweather had unwittingly led a group of suspicious miners to their secret strike. Word raced back—the Alder Gulch placers made Bannack look like a poor farm. More than 2,000 people stampeded out of town.

Bannack lived on, however, and it was named Montana's first Territorial capitol in 1864. It enjoyed

Masonic Lodge/School (1874). The school room on the first floor still seems an improvement over most modern classrooms. The Masons met upstairs.

modest economic prosperity for several years and then faded as the placers played out.

Another gold boom occurred during the 1880s and 1890s when five mechanical dredges were brought in to rework the old placer gravels along Grasshopper Creek. In 1895, the "F. L. Graves" electric dredge began operating in Bannack—the first use of such a device in North America. This resurgence was short-lived and Bannack's population quickly declined. After a long twilight, the 1930s Depression finished the place off. It was virtually abandoned by the 1940s.

Today, travelers can check in at the State Park
Visitors Center, collect a map of the town, and stroll
the dirt streets past twenty-three structures and points
of interest. About one-half the buildings which remain
date to the Territorial Period and the rest to the early
1900s. Be sure to visit Skinner's Saloon (1863) where
Henry Plummer's gang secretly met. Also worth some
time are the Meade Hotel (1875), Doc Ryburn's house,
and the log Renois cabin. Children will enjoy the
Greek Revival-style Masonic Lodge (1874) that also
served as the town school. Desks, chalk boards, and a
working merry-go-round still remain in place. On a
more sobering note, Bannack has the oldest jail in
Montana as well as a replica of the gallows where
Henry Plummer was hanged by Virginia City vigilantes
in 1864.

THE LAWLESSNESS DESCRIBED:
Vigilantes of Montana,
by Thomas Dimsdale (1953).

The smell of sagebrush and bone-dry boards is the
signature of economic collapse in the West. Sit in the
shade of Bannack and have a whiff. Despite Montana's
current population boom, you may once again catch
this scent in other transient, unplanned places across
Big Sky Country.

The Lolo Trail

THE LOLO TRAIL is a pathway leading deep into the
geography of Montana. Highway 12 parallels the route
of this trail from the town of Lolo west into Idaho.

The Nez Perce and other tribes of Idaho, Oregon,
and Washington followed this trail eastward from the
Weippe Prairie (near Orofino, Idaho) into Montana
during summer bison hunting trips to the Great
Plains. The name "Lolo" appears to have come from
the Nez Perce word for "muddy water."

The westward-bound Lewis and Clark Expedition
camped near the confluence of Lolo Creek and the
Bitterroot River on the 9th and 10th of September,
1805. They named the site "Traveller's Rest." Lewis
and Clark then headed up the Lolo Trail led by a
Shoshone woman named Pi-kee queen-ah whom they
called "Old Toby." Fallen timber, hard weather, and an

The Traveller's Rest marker beside Highway 93 south of Lolo. Betty and Cathy Wright frame the sign.

absence of game made this crossing of the Bitterroot Mountains the most arduous eleven days of their entire two-year adventure. Finally, the exhausted explorers struggled into a Nez Perce camp on the Clearwater River. The tribe fed and revived the starving whitemen, even agreeing to tend their horses while the expedition floated down the Clearwater, Snake, and Columbia rivers to Astoria and the Pacific Ocean. Lewis and Clark reached the sea on a foggy, rainy morning on 7 November 1805.

The following spring, Lewis and Clark retraced their route, gathered their horses from the Nez Perce, and headed east over Lost Trail Pass in late June. The party descended the Lolo Trail and arrived at Traveller's Rest on 30 June 1806. Here they camped for three days to plan the rest of their return trip to St. Louis.

The most wrenching story of the Lolo Trail was still to unfold.

An Indian Post Office on the Lolo Trail. Photograph
courtesy of the Montana Historical Society, Helena.

The Nez Perce Indians of Idaho and Eastern Oregon
literally had saved the Lewis and Clark Expedition in
1805, accepted missionaries in 1835, and ceded land to
the whites in 1855. But even this kindheartedness
proved inadequate to assure peace. The Salmon River
gold rush of the 1860s flooded the Nez Perce Reservation with miners who had fled the carnage of the Civil
War. By 1863, the U.S. government forced the Nez
Perce to give up thousands of acres of prime lands.
Those who accepted the small reservations were called
"treaty" Nez Perce: Those who continued to roam free
were branded as "non-treaty," outlaw bands.

By early 1877, white settlers were demanding the
forcible relocation of non-treaty Nez Perce to a reservation along the Clearwater River in Idaho. Chief
Joseph and other Nez Perce leaders attended councils
with Army General Oliver Howard. They were told
they had just thirty days to move to the Clearwater or

face violent consequences. In June, braves rode angrily off and killed several white settlers. The public cried out for retribution.

General Howard assembled a force of some 200 troopers to chase down the Nez Perce. The first fight was a rousing victory for Chief Joseph. An embarrassed Howard, whom the Indians called "General Day After Tomorrow," retaliated by attacking Chief Looking Glass's peaceful camp on the Reservation. An alliance was now forged between treaty and nontreaty bands. The Nez Perce War was on.

The Nez Perce once again defeated the Army at the Battle of the Clearwater where fewer than 100 braves had crushed Howard's expanded force of 500 soldiers. With Howard momentarily halted, Chief Joseph gathered some 800 men, women, and children and a herd of 2,000 head of livestock and raced east over the Lolo Trail toward Montana's Bitterroot Valley. Pandemonium broke out in Big Sky Country.

Colonel John Gibbon assembled soldiers and citizen volunteers at Fort Missoula. The hastily assembled "army" then road hard to Lolo Creek to confront the Nez Perce. Log barricades were quickly erected, and the men dug in for a fight. The Nez Perce chose to avoid bloodshed and simply went around these fortifications. Joseph shifted his route south and descended Mormon Creek into the Bitterroot Valley and headed south toward the Big Hole. Ever since, the Army's earthworks have been called "Fort Fizzle."

Although unused for a century, it is still possible to find portions of the Lolo Trail. The trail was actually composed of many interlacing pathways: Some have been reclaimed by nature, but others remain etched in the forest floor south of Highway 12. Bent "marker trees" and rock cairns called "Indian Post Offices" occasionally can be seen in remote areas. The Fort Fizzle site, some ten miles west of Lolo, is now just an unspectacular collection of slight depressions at a picnic and rest area on Highway 12.

The Lolo Trail and Traveller's Rest are National Historic Landmarks. The Lolo National Forest has taken some steps to leave the trail undisturbed. Yet, timber harvesting continues in many areas. The Lolo Creek Valley is being developed rapidly as a rural residential area. The Lolo Hot Springs Resort is twenty-six miles west of Lolo. Seven miles farther is the Lolo Pass cross-country ski area.

The Traveller's Rest site is a vivid reminder of the futility of mere registration as a way to conserve historic places. All that marks the site is a road sign framed by noxious weeds: A thicket of purple knapweed and yellow leafy spurge. No land has been set aside. This faded marker is surrounded by piles of logs, diesel fuel tanks, bulldozers, trailers, and a vehicle repair shop.

FOR THE WAY THINGS WERE:
Tough Trip through Paradise,
by Andrew Garcia (1967).

The Bitterroot

"THE BITTERROOT" is a mountain range, a valley, and a river. This was the first area permanently settled by Europeans in Montana. Population growth, land subdivision, and housing development are now raising grave doubts about how much of the place will retain its wild beauty.

The Bitterroot Mountains form the rugged borderline between Montana and Idaho. The main range extends south from Missoula ninety miles to Lost Trail Pass. Highway 93 runs up the Bitterroot Valley passing through a string of small towns: Lolo, Florence, Stevensville, Victor, Hamilton, and Darby. The Sapphire Mountains border the valley to the east.

The Bitterroot Mountains are composed of large masses of granitic rocks 50 to 70 million years old. Molten rock was emplaced, cooled, and crystallized three to ten miles below the surface. This 10,000-square-mile igneous intrusion is called the Idaho Batholith. Its injection caused an immense mass of overlying billion-year-old quartzite and argillite (a shale-like rock) to rise. This so-called Sapphire Block sheared away and slid more than twenty miles eastward on low-angle thrust faults. It came to rest as the Sapphire Mountains. The entire front of the Bitterroot

Range dips about twenty-five degrees eastward. From many vantage points, it looks like a ramp, which is what it was. The shear zone was altered by heat and pressure and contains platy metamorphic rocks called mylonite gneiss.

Most of the rugged features of the Bitterroot Mountains were formed by Pleistocene glaciation when a vast ice cap covered the high country. Peaks such as Lolo (9,075 feet), St. Mary's (9,331 feet), El Capitan (9,920 feet), and Trapper (10,157 feet) stood above the ice. Valley glaciers moved downslope carving textbook u-shaped canyons with smooth granite walls. Blodgett Canyon near Hamilton is a classic example of this type of terrain. Today, much of the spectacular high country is contained in the 1,337,910-acre (2,090-square-mile) Selway-Bitterroot Wilderness Area. Grizzly bears may soon be reintroduced into the wilderness after an absence of more than sixty years. Hunters killed off the last griz in the mid-1930s.

The Bitterroot glaciers descended to an elevation of about 4,000 feet. Hummocky piles of debris called moraines were deposited at valley mouths where ice sheets melted. During the Ice Age, Glacial Lake Missoula periodically filled the Bitterroot Valley and other Western Montana basins when the Clark Fork River was block by ice sheets at Sand Point, Idaho, some 200 miles downstream of Missoula. During lake-filling cycles, Bitterroot glaciers calved off icebergs that drifted across the water.

The Bitterroot River is a braided (anastomosing) and meandering waterway. Channel changes happen each spring, and river guides must constantly relearn the river. The black cottonwood and ponderosa pine floodplain contains numerous spring creeks and sloughs. Whitetail deer, foxes, and myriads of ducks and geese use these prime wetland habitats. Bald eagles and osprey patrol the river, hunting trout.

In 1993, several huge mudslides tumbled down slopes in Overwhich Creek (in the West Fork of the Bitterroot). The U.S. Forest Service allowed the forests to be clearcut, and a rainstorm brought the

Opposite top: St. Mary's Mission in Stevensville.

Opposite below: The Daly Mansion outside of Hamilton on the Eastside Highway. Copper generated far more wealth in Montana than did gold and silver.

unprotected mountainside down. The Overwhich Creek bull trout population was buried in silt and destroyed. Silt poured down the Bitterroot adversely affecting the trout fishery for months. Despite this damage, clearcutting persists in parts of the Bitterroot watershed.

Long before all the fly fishing buffs arrived, the Bitterroot Valley was called "the Salish Land." In 1841, Jesuit priest Pierre DeSmet established St. Mary's Mission just north of present-day Stevensville. Twelve structures were erected to form Montana's first "town." Wheat, oats, vegetables, and cattle were raised. A flour mill processed the grains. Indians were converted to Catholicism. In 1850, Father DeSmet was called away, and the Mission lands were sold to John Owen for $250. Owen built an adobe fort on the site which is now a state Historic Monument. The adobe walls, bastions, and houses are gone, but portions of the old dormitory remain. The St. Mary's Mission in Stevensville was built in 1866 by Father Anthony Ravalli, for whom Ravalli County is named.

Agriculture has long been one of the mainstays of life in the valley. In 1910, the Bitterroot Irrigation District was formed. Water was diverted from Lake Como (north of Darby) into a twenty-foot wide, seventy-five-mile long canal known as the "Big Ditch" that was constructed along the benchlands on the east side of the valley. This irrigation project led to the "Apple Boom" of 1910 to 1917 when more than 75,000 acres were planted into Mackintosh and crab apples. Settlers were drawn in by the lure of an idyllic, rural lifestyle. Thousands bought land for as much as $1,000 per acre but soon went broke and left. Markets proved to be too far away. By the 1920s, the apple industry had disappeared, and the orchards were abandoned. Cattle ranches, dairy farms, and grain operations became the main agricultural pursuits.

Today, the Bitterroot is being transformed from an agrarian landscape into a crowded suburb of Missoula, lying north in the Clark Fork Valley. In the 1960s, Ravalli County had one of the state's highest percentages of "native Montanans." It is now has the lowest

The land development boom in the Bitterroot Valley and the rest of Montana is not a subtle process.

percentage, about 40%. The 1970s saw a subdivision boom that went bust in the 1980s. The 1990s have seen a 22% increase in population; mostly migrants from congested, crime-ravaged cities in California, Oregon, and Washington. Ravalli County has grown from 14,409 residents in 1970 to more than 33,000 in 1998. It is the second fastest growing county in the state behind Flathead (Kalispell).

The north end of the valley has experienced most of the growth in places such as Florence and Stevensville (locally called "Stevi"). Commuting to Missoula has caused traffic on Highway 93 to double in ten years. The roadway will soon be rebuilt as a four-lane interstate highway. Hamilton, in the south end of the valley, has grown into a trade center with 4,000 residents. Its surrounding agricultural land, scenic open space, and key wildlife habitats are quickly being converted to homesites. Even copper king Marcus Daly's 28,000-acre showplace, the Bitterroot Stock Farm, is being subdivided for residential development. The forty-two-room Daly Mansion is open to visitors during the summer months. Recently, local vigilantes known as the "Montana Militia" and the "Freemen" have reacted to the changes by arming themselves and threatening judges, land-use planners, and other officials.

The Bitterroot embodies all the salient traits of modern Montana: Endangered beauty, threatened peacefulness, a soaring cost of living, and shrinking wages. The geography of Montana is infused with the stories of such places, of boom and bust and conflicts over the land. Only now the changes come with increasing speed. And the responsibilities of maintaining the good life in Big Sky Country have grown enormous.

FOR THE FULL RANGE OF MONTANA VOICES: *The Last Best Place: A Montana Anthology,* edited by William Kittredge and Annick Smith (1988).

The Big Hole

THE BIG HOLE VALLEY southwest of Butte, is a landscape of broad margins and sobering reminders. It is a place of immense ranches, lush hay meadows, and hard memories.

For centuries, the Nez Perce Indians of Idaho entered this basin along the Nee-Me-Poo Trail to dig the nutritious roots of the blue camas that flourished in wet meadows along the Big Hole River. Many tribes also traversed the valley on their way to hunt bison in the herds that blackened the Great Plains to the east. The Lewis and Clark Expedition passed through the valley at the site of Wisdom on 6 August 1805. Meriwether Lewis observed that "the bed of the river, which is now overflown with water in many places, spreads through old channels with their bottoms covered with grass." The multi-channeled (anastomosing) river was bordered by willow thickets alive with beaver. Arctic grayling thrived in the frigid, clear water.

Over the years, a few fur trappers ventured into the valley and named it the "Big Hole." To these musky, high-smelling pelt hunters, deep structural basins surrounded by high glaciated peaks were often called a "hole." Jackson Hole in northwest Wyoming, south of Yellowstone Park, is the best known of these. The Big Hole is framed by the Pioneer Mountains to the east, the Anaconda Pintler Mountains to the north, and the Beaverhead (West Big Hole) Mountains to the west.

Conflicts between migratory Indian bands and seasonal white trappers and prospectors were rare in the early 1800s. Winter temperatures of 30 to 40 degrees below zero Fahrenheit secured the aching isolation of the valley. Even the golden eagles, prairie falcons, spotted sandpipers, Canada geese, mallards, and cinnamon teals abandoned the Big Hole in the depth of winter. The only sound was harsh wind blowing across crusted snow and sagebrush.

The silence ended in 1877. During the Nez Perce War, Chief Joseph's contingent of 800 men, women, and children headed east from Idaho seeking refuge among the Crow tribe of Eastern Montana. The Nez Perce evaded federal troops from Fort Missoula along the Lolo Trail and headed south through the Bitterroot Valley leaving hundreds of white homesteaders unharmed. The exhausted Indians finally climbed Chief Joseph Pass and entered the Big Hole Valley to camp. Believing that the Army was days behind them, they erected tipis and slept.

Colonel John Gibbon's ragtag force of 200 soldiers and Missoula citizens, however, were riding close on the heels of the Nez Perce. At sunrise on 9 August 1877, Colonel Gibbon looked down at the North Fork of the Big Hole River and saw the slumbering Indian encampment. He quickly mounted a surprise attack. Dozens of Nez Perce were killed in their tipis during the opening salvo. The Nez Perce braves rallied, captured the Army's howitzer, and began picking off soldiers one by one. The siege continued for thirty-six hours until the Army was in such disarray that the Nez Perce could organize a retreat southward. Although the Indians killed thirty men under Gibbon's command, they lost eighty-nine tribal members—most of them women and children.

The Big Hole: Haystacks and high peaks.

The fleeing Nez Perce traveled hundreds of miles over the next two months. The band walked through Yellowstone National Park (established in 1872) and the Absaroka Mountains before finally surrendering at the Battle of the Bear Paw in north-central Montana. It was here on October 5th that Chief Joseph was reported to have said: "It is cold and we have no blankets. The little children are freezing to death . . . Hear me, my chiefs! I am tired. My heart is sick and sad. From where the sun now stands, I will fight no more forever."

The Big Hole National Battlefield is beside Highway 43 west of Wisdom. The Visitors Center contains displays and recreations of the Big Hole fight. The only way to feel the power of this tragedy is to walk along the placid riverside to the Nez Perce camp site. Bare

The beaverslide hay stacker is the vernacular signature of the Big Hole.

Puttin' up hay in the Big Hole. A beaverslide hay stacker in operation: Hay is piled onto sliding tines, raised by pulleys to the top, and dumped onto the growing stack.

tipi poles lacking skin covers rise into the cobalt sky. Markers show where Indians and soldiers fell. Sit and listen to the water. Imagine the gunfire and terror that broke that morning. Remember that to this day the Nez Perce live in poverty on small reservations. You are not sitting on an historic site but on a living piece of geography, a sacred portion of the continuing culture of American Indians. The Nez Perce still come here each year to remember their dead and the loss of a generous landscape.

Driving through the Big Hole Valley today you can see the mixed legacy of what came next. Ranching began around Wisdom and Jackson in 1882. The evidence of stewardship is seen in the verdant flood-irrigated hay meadows and abundant sandhill cranes, eagles, and waterfowl. Blue camas still grow. The Big Hole is the home of the "beaverslide hay stacker." Montanans call it the "Land of 10,000 Hay Stacks." The air is so dry and cold that hay is stacked out in the open before being fed to Hereford and Angus cattle in the winter.

Yet, when winter snowpacks are low or summer droughts are prolonged, irrigation withdrawals markedly reduce the flow of the Big Hole River. This threatens fluvial arctic grayling populations which are found in the lower forty-eight states only in the Big Hole. Several "conservation easements" have been placed on local ranches to prevent housing development, mining, and other land uses which would threaten this rare fish.

The Big Hole Valley reminds us of many things. Beneath the beautiful scenery are stories of racial intolerance, environmental exploitation, agricultural stewardship and the promise of landscape conservation. This is a remote, astonishing valley with a small population of clannish ranch families. Wisdom sits in the bottom of the "hole" at 6,133 feet and often claims the nationwide low temperature—year round. In summer, clouds of mosquitoes attack those daring to venture outside their cars. Jobs are nonexistent for newcomers. The Big Hole is a place for visiting, not for settling.

TO LEARN THE WAY OF LIFE: *Making Hay*, by Verlyn Klinkenborg (1986), and *The Mountain West: Interpreting the Folk Landscape*, by Terry G. Jordan, Jon T. Kilpinen, and Charles F. Gritzner (1996).

Anaconda

ANACONDA IS A TOWN created for one vital purpose—to smelt copper ore.

Today, all that remains of the Anaconda Company era is the 585-foot-tall brick smokestack on the south side of town at the foot of the Pintler Mountains. The remainder of the Washoe Smelter complex was torn down for scrap in the early 1980s by the Atlantic Richfield Corporation (ARCO). Residents of Anaconda now work at local retail, professional, logging, and manufacturing jobs, or they commute twenty miles to Butte. Many of the modest pink, turquoise, and yellow houses set on tiny, well-tended lots are owned by retired smelter workers. Despite the loss of the town's founding industry, Anaconda still has 10,278 loyal residents.

The 585-foot-tall Washoe smokestack is all that remains of the copper smelter at Anaconda. To some, the stack is an industrial eyesore. Yet, local residents successfully fought to save it. For them, the stack is an elegant and meaningful sculpture and a reminder of the past. For them, it is Montana's Statue of Liberty.

Anaconda is a pleasant middle-class community with nice parks and an active historic preservation effort. The old depot for Marcus Daly's ore hauling trains at 300 West Commercial Street is now a Visitors Center. The Washoe Theater, St. Marks Episcopal Church, Hearst Free Library, Deer Lodge County Courthouse, and the Barich, Davidson, and Durston blocks are all listed on the National Register of Historic Places. These and other fascinating structures are scattered along Main and Park streets. Sadly, the architectural integrity of the Marcus Daly Hotel was destroyed by a misguided renovation effort that removed the top floor. Stores now fill the remaining space. In many ways, neighborhood saloons such as the Club Moderne and JFK Bar best capture the feeling of Anaconda.

A new golf course designed by Jack Nicklaus has been built at the "Old Works" Superfund Site. These are the first links built on toxic waste in America. The sand traps are filled with copper slag.

The present smelter stack is not the first one built in Anaconda. In 1884, mining entrepreneur Marcus Daly, using San Francisco capitalists' money, erected the Anaconda Reduction Works north of town along Warm Springs Creek and platted the townsite for his workers. This facility had twin blast furnaces that could roast and smelt 500 tons of ore per day. Air pollution immediately began to kill the surrounding forests and to damage nearby ranchlands. In 1902, Daly moved the operation to an area south of town which came to be known simply as "The Hill." The first stack measured 225 feet tall and was fueled by 300,000 cords of wood per year taken from the region's mountainsides. Downwind in the Deer Lodge Valley, thousands of cattle were killed, and crop yields plummeted in the smelter's cloud of ash, fluoride, sulphur, arsenic, and heavy metals. The Deer Lodge Farmers Association sued the company, and Daly responded by raising the stack to 300 feet in height. The fumes only damaged more of the landscape. Anaconda eventually bought out many ranchers under the urging of President Teddy Roosevelt.

Black slag heaps loom over Highway 1. Re-vegetated slag in the background forms a sharp contrast. Topsoil was imported, grass seed was dispersed, and irrigation systems were used to stabilize the waste.

In 1918, the present stack was completed. It was once the tallest in the world and remains the most massive in volume. The stack weighs 33,000 tons, contains 2,466,392 bricks of different sizes, and has a base made of 5,000 cubic feet of reinforced concrete. The top measures sixty feet across—a school bus could be dropped down it. At full capacity the Washoe Smelter released 4 million cubic feet of toxic emissions per minute through this titanic stack. A zone of dead and dying vegetation extended outward in all directions. Trees were killed above town and as far as ten miles away at Georgetown Lake, the company's industrial reservoir. The hillsides are still bare in many places. The former grasslands east of town look like a desert with sand dunes, scattered shrubs, and weeds. Partially reclaimed black slag heaps border Highway 1.

The Warm Springs Ponds beside Interstate 90 were built early in the twentieth century as cachement basins for contaminated runoff from smelting operations. Ironically, since the closure of the Washoe Smelter, the ponds have stabilized and are one of the regions most important waterfowl habitats. The ponds, Silver Bow Creek, and much of the smelting complex are now federal Superfund cleanup sites.

The copper era left behind a mixed legacy in Montana. Jobs were created and families were raised. Copper helped win two world wars. Homes and countless products could not have been built without the tough people of no nonsense towns such as Anaconda and Butte. Yet, in the 1970s, the Anaconda Company sold out, and ARCO closed it down. Thousands of workers were laid off. The entire state suffered economically. And the landscape may never be the same.

PUTTING IT IN PERSPECTIVE:
Twentieth-Century Montana:
A State of Extremes,
by K. Ross Toole (1972).

The Missouri Breaks

THE MISSOURI BREAKS is a deeply dissected and profoundly remote landscape paralleling the Missouri River in Central Montana. It is called a "breaks" because the flat grasslands have been broken into countless ravines. This is a semi-arid place of sandstone and shale carved by cloudbursts and river floods into good measures of beauty

This expansive part of the state is a mosaic of short-grass steppes and prairie dog towns, strips of dryland wheat, and circles of sandy buttes. The Breaks extends westward along the Missouri from the Charles M. Russell and UL Bend national wildlife refuges (and UL Bend Wilderness) to Fort Benton. Large portions of this area have been designated the Missouri National Wild and Scenic River corridor. The Lewis and Clark National Historic Trail is contained within this protected area. In 1805, the explorers boated up what the French called the "River Longue" trying to locate the mythical Northwest Passage for President Thomas Jefferson.

The Missouri Breaks is made of much more than prickly pear cactus and muddy water. Many Indian nations hunted bison here in the days before whites arrived. During the 1870s and 1880s, this was a lair for renegades, wolf hunters, fugitives, murderers, and worse. Cattle rustlers wreaked havoc on herds, often hiding out in the Breaks before trailing the stolen animals north to Canadian markets. Even the law knew enough to steer clear of thousands of side-canyons stretched out across the Breaks. Once the times grew safer, this tough land was used as open cattle range. Today, the Breaks is one of the state's most precious wildlife areas.

Up to five million mallard, pintail, canvasback, redhead, shoveler, green-winged teal, American widgeon, and gadwall ducks pass through the Missouri Breaks during their spring and fall migrations. Whistling swans grace the riversides. Canada, snow, and Ross' geese rely on the Missouri River as a resting place on their long journeys between the Arctic and Central and South America. Prairie falcons and numerous hawks hunt the grasslands and coulees for ground squirrels. Bald eagles and osprey snag fish from the river. Odd, ancient paddlefish patrol the cloudy depths sensing their environment through long, flat noses. Paddlefish can reach eight feet long and can weigh more than 300 pounds.

The Breaks is Montana's "Outback." In 175 Missouri River miles, there is only one paved road that crosses the water, Route 191 between Lewistown and Malta. Two other bridges serve rough gravel roads. There are no motels, gas stations, stores, or espresso bars out here. Free ferry service is provided by the state at three sites: McClelland, Loma, and Virgelle. These ferries operate from spring through fall and only at certain hours.

FOR GOOD PHOTOGRAPHY AND
ELEGANT DESCRIPTION:
Montana's Missouri River,
Montana Geographic Series
(1979).

The Missouri Breaks is not a theme park. Float trips are popular with people willing to rough it. Rattlesnakes have been known to swim out to greet passing boats. It would be wise to dissuade them from coming aboard.

Opposite and above: **A classic "breaks" landscape within the Missouri Wild and Scenic River corridor. Photographs courtesy of the Montana Department of Commerce: Travel Montana.**

Makoshika Badlands

"BADLANDS" IS AN ODD NAME for a landscape so intensely beautiful as Makoshika State Park located off Interstate 94 adjacent to Glendive. The early French fur traders referred to these intricately dissected areas as *mauvais terres pour traverser*, or "bad lands for travel." Modern Westerners also tend to dismiss places which can't feed a cow as being bad country. Yet, Sioux hunters even called this chaotic landscape "Ma-ko'-shi-ka," which roughly translates as "Hell cooled over."

Makoshika is a maze of eroded hills and coulees reminiscent of Badlands National Park in South Dakota. But the shale, sandstone, and mudstone strata of Makoshika contain an even more fascinating memoir of the earth.

About 70 million years ago, late in the Cretaceous Period, the North American tectonic plate was in the tropics. At that time, this part of Montana was a moist, warm lowland where mud accumulated in river floodplains and swamps formed next to retreating seas. Lush vegetation covered the land. The heavy steps of Tyrannosaurus rex, Triceratops, and other dinosaurs made the earth shake. The bones of countless generations of dinosaurs were covered by silt and clay which hardened into rock now called the Hellcreek Shale.

One day the rules changed. A gigantic asteroid struck the Earth, possibly in the Gulf of Mexico off Yucatan. This sent an immense cloud of dust high into the atmosphere blocking most of the sun's rays. Plants began to die, and the dinosaurs were swept into a furious worldwide struggle to survive. Once their food chains collapsed, the "thunder lizards" became extinct. Scientists have named this asteroid "Nemesis" or simply "the Death Star." Mammals began to dominate the planet. In some parts of the world, a layer of iridium (an element related to platinum) has been found at the geologic boundary between Cretaceous and Tertiary time. Iridium is rare on Earth but common on asteroids.

Opposite: **Makoshika Badlands is a place of shifting patterns of light.**

Millions of years of rain and wind have carved the rocks of Makoshika into classic badlands topography. The sparsity of junipers and grasses is due to aridity, past fires, and the instability of rapidly eroding hillsides. It is a place of elegant geomorphology where windstorms, flash floods, landslides, mudflows, and slumps continue to create ever-changing landforms. At overlooks, the deeply eroded rocks take on the form of pinnacles, castle turrets, pedestals, potatoes, pyramids, and domes. Sit awhile and enjoy the terrestrial equivalent of cloud gazing.

Makoshika State Park has a Visitors Center (with displays of fossils), camping facilities, and several hiking trails throughout its 8,123 acres. The one-half mile Cap Rock Nature Trail has exhibits and a self-guiding leaflet. The Park's dirt road from Radio Hill Junction to Artists' Vista Point is steep, eroded, and not recommended for large or low-clearance vehicles or for the faint of heart. The April turkey vulture migration is a must for birders.

The region surrounding Makoshika State Park is marked by extensive development of oil, gas, and coal resources. Inside this protected area, amateur geologists will always be able to encounter fossil dinosaur bones, leaf imprints, pine cone casts, cephalopods, and other fossils. It is illegal to dig in the sediments or to collect anything. This is a dinosaur burial ground. Show some respect. These marvelous creatures dominated Earth for 100 million years. Human industrial society is about 200 years old.

FOR THE GEOLOGY:
Roadside Geology of Montana,
by David Alt and
Donald W. Hyndman (1986).

The Missile Silo Landscape

THE ROLLING WHEAT FIELDS and rangelands surrounding Great Falls contain an unnerving surprise: 200 nuclear missile silos. This represents one-fifth of the U.S. ground-based nuclear weapons force. The rest are located within five large Intercontinental Ballistic Missile (ICBM) clusters spread over the states of North and South Dakota, Wyoming, Nebraska, Colorado, and Missouri.

The atomic bombs and the rockets designed to deliver them are housed in thick bunkers made of fortified concrete and metal. The exact locations of these silos are hardly a national secret, however. Each is located in plain sight next to public roads in a swath extending 150 miles east from Augusta to Grass Range.

The weapons are arranged in a series of clusters known as "Flights" that are labeled A through T. Each Flight consists of a launch control center and ten missile silos. A silo can be identified by a roadside marker such as K3 or D10. Each is accessed by a gated dirt road and is enclosed by chain-link fences topped with barbed wire. No guard posts can be seen. Heavily-armed Air Force personnel sitting below ground monitor the perimeter for signs of intrusion. At no time should these fortresses be approached. Anti-

The **"Humankind Booby-Trapped" nuclear missile silo near Simms on Highway 200. As a crow flies, Ulm Pishkun is only twenty-two miles east of this site.**

Enough said.

nuclear activists have on occasion cut fences, damaged silo warning systems, and made symbolic peace gestures such as sowing wheat seeds across the missile exit portals. Arrests have followed.

Nukewatch and other anti-nuclear groups have assigned names to each of the remaining 1,000 missile silos in the United States. Names such as Starving Millions, Fat Buffalo, Bomb Bordello, and Molten Bones are among the names encountered in Montana. The "Humankind Booby-Trapped" silo (H7) is located 1.8 miles south of Simms on Highway 200. The "Radiation Sickness" silo (C11) is one mile northwest of Stanford on Highway 87. The A1 or "Mountain Life Community" launch control is on the left side of the road 3.9 miles west of Raynesford on Highway 87. This was the first operational Minuteman ICBM silo in America. It "came on line" in 1962 and was President Kennedy's trump card during the Cuban Missile Crisis. The A5 ("Siksikauw") missile silo is found deep in the Lewis and Clark National Forest. Air Force personnel report hauntings by an Indian spirit.

The missile silo landscape is Montana's most unimaginable place. Many of these Minuteman III silos are situated in rolling fertile farmland near such small towns as Winifred, Denton, Conrad, and Judith Gap. The views toward the Rocky Mountain Front and the Little Belt Mountains are astonishing. It all seems like Peace on Earth. Yet, this is the geography of "Ground Zero." In the event of thermonuclear war, everything in this portion of the state would become irradiated dust.

WHERE THE MISSILES ARE: *Nuclear Heartland*, edited by Samuel H. Day, Jr. (1988), and *Nuclear Landscapes*, by Peter Goin (1991).

Montana's missile silos are its ultimate roadside attraction.

Red Rock Lakes and Refuge

RED ROCK LAKES in southwest Montana's Centennial Valley is one of America's most important waterfowl and wildlife sanctuaries.

These lakes and the surrounding wetlands and meadows are a key component of the national wildlife refuge program begun by President Theodore Roosevelt in 1903. Most early reserves were set aside to protect a key species. Later, conserving migratory habitats, breeding areas, wintering sites, and larger ecosystems became the guiding principles of the system. Red Rocks is no exception. This is a refuge where the trumpeter swan was saved from extinction, and scores of other species now nest in peace.

Commercial hunting almost wiped out the trumpeters. Between 1853 and 1877, the Hudson's Bay Company sold 17,671 swan skins; nearly all of these were trumpeters. These graceful, white-feathered

A mated pair of trumpeter swans at the Red Rock Lakes. Photograph courtesy of the Montana Department of Commerce: Travel Montana.

creatures once ranged from Seattle to Chicago and numbered in the tens of thousands. By 1919, only a few breeding pairs were known to exist in the United States. Biologists feared the species would soon become extinct. Amazingly, in 1932, a colony of twenty-six swans was found in the Centennial Valley. Congress acted to save the birds and formed the Red Rock Lakes National Wildlife Refuge in 1935. This 42,525-acre refuge is now home to a flock of 300 trumpeter swans. Despite federal laws protecting them, only 600 members of the species exist in the entire nation.

The Red Rock Lakes refuge can be reached by driving twenty-five miles east from the Monida Exit on Interstate 15 or by a rough gravel road crossing Red Rock Pass (7,120 feet) from Henry's Lake in Idaho. South of Upper Red Rock Lake is an unimproved campground. No other tourist facilities exist, since much of the refuge is also a designated wilderness area. Upper and Lower Red Rock lakes are surrounded by extensive wetlands. Mosquito repellant is a must.

Yet, for those wishing to observe wildlife quietly, the trip is rewarding. The trumpeter swans are present in the region year-round. Adults have snowy-white plumage and elegantly-curved necks. They glide across the water and upend themselves to feed on aquatic plants. In the spring, the trumpeters nest in marshlands building huge nests of sedges, bulrushes, and grass. Mated pairs establish and defend territories 70 to 150 acres in size. Four to five eggs per clutch are typical. The young swans, called cygnets, grow from seven ounces to nineteen pounds in only nine weeks. They take flight only fifteen weeks after hatching.

Trumpeter swans share this astounding habitat with a grand array of other water birds. Thousands of lesser snow geese and Canada geese arrive during spring and fall migrations. Immense numbers of duck species also utilize the refuge, including mallard, pintail, American widgeon, gadwall, blue-winged teal, green-winged teal, canvasback, redhead, lesser scaup, harlequin, bufflehead, and Barrow's goldeneye. Grizzly bears move through the Centennial Valley on forays between the Centennial Mountains and Yellowstone National Park. Red foxes can often be seen hunting for mice, ground squirrels, and bird eggs. Bald and golden eagles are sighted regularly.

America has lost more than half its wetlands to development. Places such as the Red Rock Lakes are critical portions of our national landscape. Stand by the lakes at dusk. Listen to the calls of the trumpeter swans echo across the water like a French horn concerto. It is the sound of a conservation success story. It is the sound of the original America.

BIRDS AND MORE BIRDS:
Ducks, Geese and Swans of North America,
by Frank C. Bellrose (1980).

JOHN B. WRIGHT has lived and worked in Montana since 1973. He is the author of *Montana Ghost Dance: Essays on Land and Life* (1998) and *Rocky Mountain Divide: Selling and Saving the West,* which in 1994 won the J. B. Jackson Prize, given by the Association of American Geographers, and the Geographical Society of Chicago's Publication Award. Dr. Wright resides in Missoula, Montana, where he serves on the Board of the Five Valleys Land Trust. He is also an associate professor of geography at New Mexico State University.

THE NEW MEXICO GEOGRAPHICAL SOCIETY, legendary society of the American West, is a nonprofit organization dedicated to the public welfare. It fosters the discovery and dissemination of geographical knowledge far and wide through public lectures, regional and international conferences, educational field seminars, research, and publications designed to reach the student, scholar, and general reader. Its headquarters are in La Mesilla, the historic community in southern New Mexico that was under the jurisdiction of the Mexican State of Chihuahua until the 1854 acquisition of the Gadsden Purchase Territory by the United States. For information about membership, events, and Society publications, please write:

The New Mexico Geographical Society, Inc.
P. O. Box 1201
Mesilla, New Mexico 88046-1201
U.S.A.